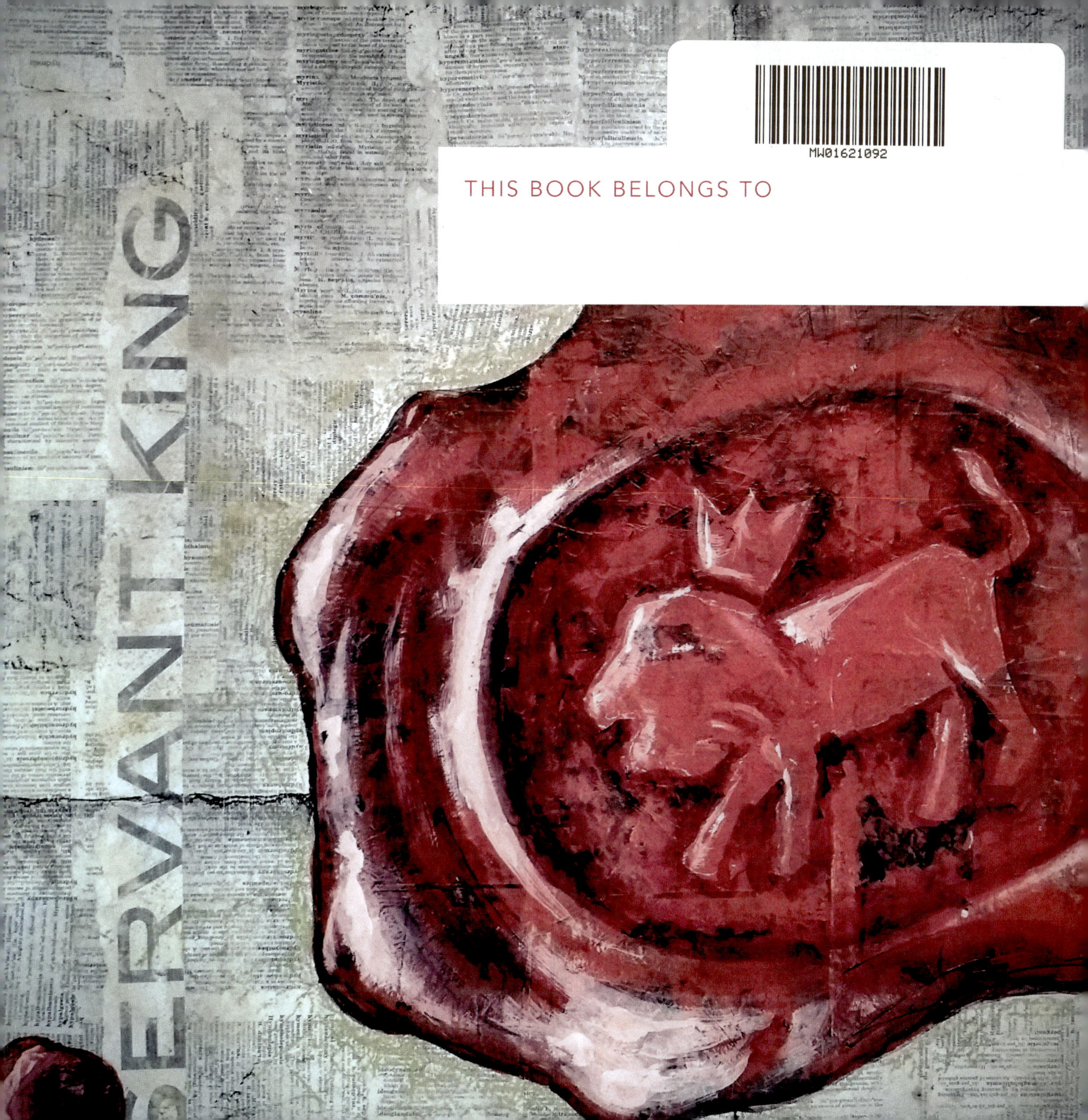
ERVANT KING
MW01621092
THIS BOOK BELONGS TO

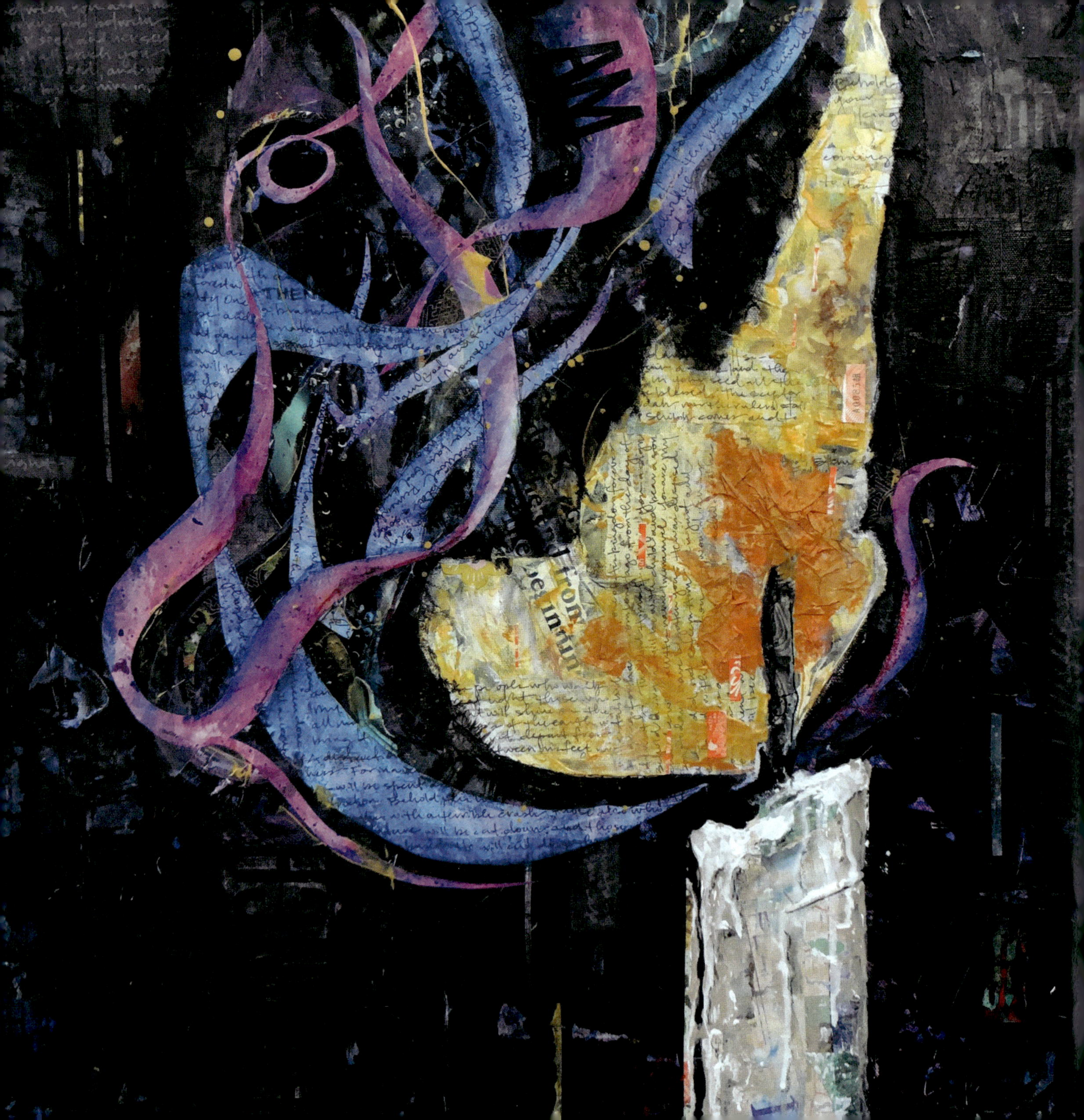
AM

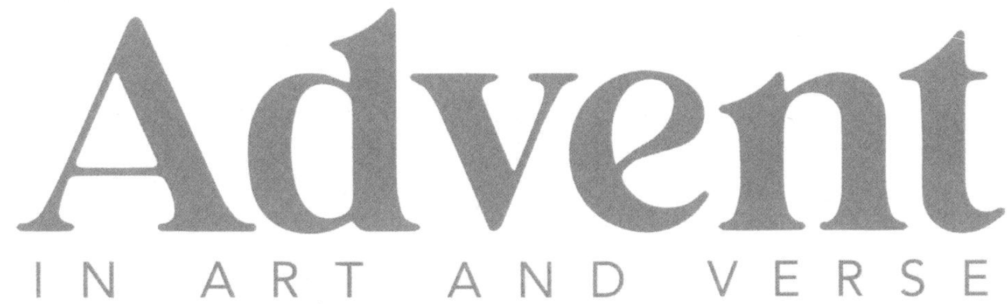

RIKI YARBROUGH

Advent in Art and Verse

Artwork, poetry, and design by Riki Yarbrough

ISBN-13: 978-0-9996981-2-9

art

MATTHEW 1:1-16

The book of the genealogy of Jesus Christ, the son of David, the son of Abraham.

ABRAHAM was the father of Isaac, and **ISAAC** the father of Jacob, and **JACOB** the father of Judah and his brothers, and **JUDAH** the father of Perez and Zerah by Tamar, and Perez the father of Hezron, and Hezron the father of Ram, and Ram the father of Amminadab, and Amminadab the father of Nahshon, and Nahshon the father of Salmon, and Salmon the father of Boaz by **RAHAB**, and **BOAZ** the father of Obed by **RUTH**, and Obed the father of Jesse, and **JESSE** the father of David the king.

And **DAVID** was the father of Solomon by the wife of Uriah, and **SOLOMON** the father of Rehoboam, and **REHOBOAM** the father of Abijah, and **ABIJAH** the father of Asaph, and **ASAPH** the father of Jehoshaphat, and **JEHOSHAPHAT** the father of Joram, and **JORAM** the father of Uzziah, and **UZZIAH** the father of Jotham, and **JOTHAM** the father of Ahaz, and **AHAZ** the father of Hezekiah, and **HEZEKIAH** the father of Manasseh, and **MANASSEH** the father of Amos, and **AMON** the father of Josiah, and **JOSIAH** the father of Jechoniah and his brothers, at the time of the **DEPORTATION TO BABYLON**.

And after the deportation to Babylon: **JECHONIAH** was the father of Shealtiel, and Shealtiel the father of Zerubbabel, and **ZERUBBABEL** the father of Abiud, and Abiud the father of Eliakim, and Eliakim the father of Azor, and Azor the father of Zadok, and Zadok the father of Achim, and Achim the father of Eliud, and Eliud the father of Eleazar, and Eleazar the father of Matthan, and Matthan the father of Jacob, and Jacob the father of **JOSEPH** the husband of **MARY**, of whom **JESUS** was born, who is called Christ.

GOD
ADAM & EVE
CAIN & ABEL
ENOCH
NOAH
ABRAHAM
ISAAC
JACOB
JOSEPH
JUDAH
MOSES
RAHAB
BOAZ & RUTH
JESSE
DAVID
SOLOMON
EVIL KINGS
ISAIAH
GOOD KINGS
CAPTIVITY
ZERUBBABEL
PROPHECY
SILENCE
ZECHARIAH
MARY
JOSEPH
JESUS

LUKE 3:23-38

JESUS, when he began his ministry, was about thirty years of age, being the son (as was supposed) of **JOSEPH**, the son of Heli, the son of Matthat, the son of Levi, the son of Melchi, the son of Jannai, the son of Joseph, the son of Mattathias, the son of Amos, the son of Nahum, the son of Esli, the son of Naggai, the son of Maath, the son of Mattathias, the son of Semein, the son of Josech, the son of Joda, the son of Joanan, the son of Rhesa, the son of **ZERUBBABEL**, the son of Shealtiel, the son of Neri, the son of Melchi, the son of Addi, the son of Cosam, the son of Elmadam, the son of Er, the son of Joshua, the son of Eliezer, the son of Jorim, the son of Matthat, the son of Levi, the son of Simeon, the son of Judah, the son of Joseph, the son of Jonam, the son of Eliakim, the son of Melea, the son of Menna, the son of Mattatha, the son of Nathan, the son of **DAVID**, the son of **JESSE**, the son of Obed, the son of **BOAZ**, the son of Sala, the son of Nahshon, the son of Amminadab, the son of Admin, the son of Arni, the son of Hezron, the son of Perez, the son of **JUDAH**, the son of **JACOB**, the son of **ISAAC** , the son of **ABRAHAM**, the son of Terah, the son of Nahor, the son of Serug, the son of Reu, the son of Peleg, the son of Eber, the son of Shelah, the son of Cainan, the son of Arphaxad, the son of Shem, the son of **NOAH**, the son of Lamech, the son of Methuselah, the son of **ENOCH**, the son of Jared, the son of Mahalaleel, the son of Cainan, the son of Enos, the son of Seth, the son of **ADAM**, the son of **GOD**.

**Circled names are not in the lineage of Christ, but are included to provide necessary context.*

table of contents

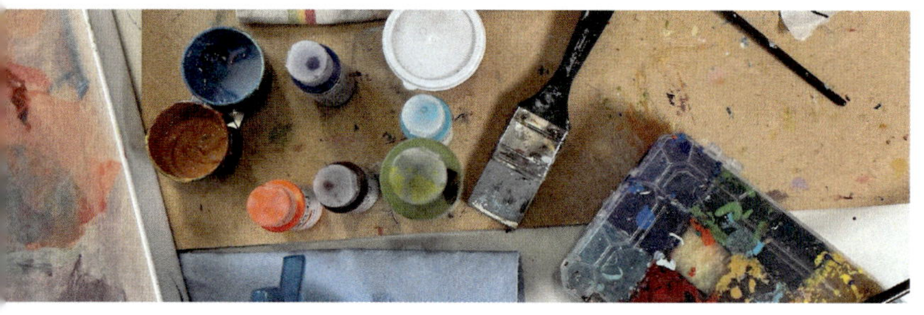

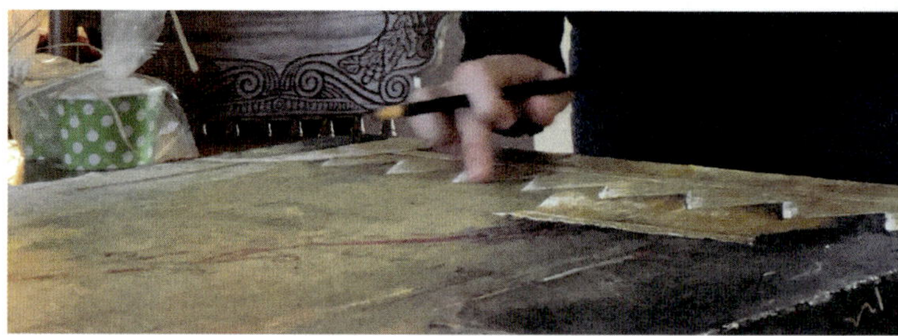

introduction

It was the images that first enticed me to study the lineage of Christ. The ornaments dangled from a Christmas tree and each bore a symbol that represented a part of "Jesse's tree"—an apple for Adam and Eve, a rainbow for Noah, stars for Abraham, wedding bands for Boaz and Ruth, a shepherd's crook for David. As a graphic designer, I'm a sucker for icons, where an entire narrative is packed into a single, simple image. These were all chapters to a larger story. In addition to the symbols, however, it was the name of this story-telling tradition that intrigued me most: *Jesse's Tree*. It led me to a treasure hunt in the Scriptures.

> Behold, the Lord God of hosts
> will lop the boughs with terrifying power;
> the great in height will be hewn down,
> and the lofty will be brought low.
> He will cut down the thickets of the forest with an axe,
> and Lebanon will fall by the Majestic One.
> *There shall come forth a shoot from the stump of Jesse,*
> *and a branch from his roots shall bear fruit.*
> (Isaiah 10:33-34; 11:1 ESV, emphasis added)

As I combed through Isaiah's prophecies, many of my questions were answered, but it sparked an investigation into some of the most over-looked passages in Scripture —the genealogies of Christ in the Gospels of Matthew and Luke. I followed each name listed to where his or her story was told in the Old Testament and New. This personal study eventually spilled over onto my family until it soaked every day of the Advent season, from Thanksgiving to Christmas morning. For each of those 27 days, we focused on a specific person or event noted in the Messiah's line and retold that story —that particular part of Jesse's tree— to move us one step closer to His coming. From His first spoken word in Genesis 1 to the day of His birth in Luke 2, following all the twists and turns in between, we anticipated Jesus' advent.

In November of 2018, an idea took root in my mind as I prepared for the season. *What if every morning I set aside time to tell His story on canvas?*

I'm a mixed media artist. It is through building layers of acrylic paint and paper that I visually tell a story. A painting usually requires meticulously working through ideas, walking away and returning, adding and subtracting, until at some point beauty emerges through the chaos. The process is slow for me, taking several days or weeks. But here I was, at the start of the busiest time of the year, compelled

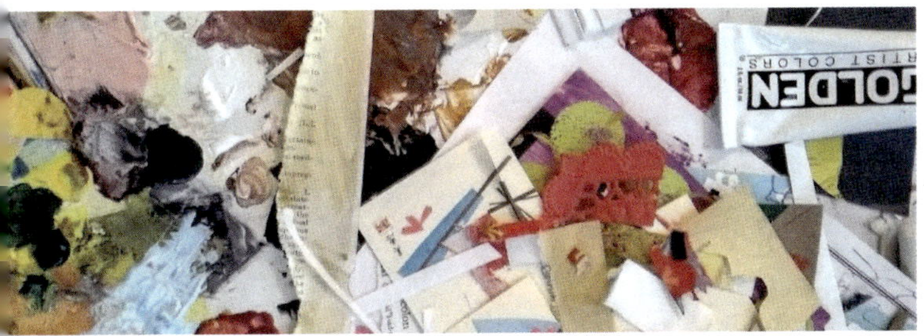

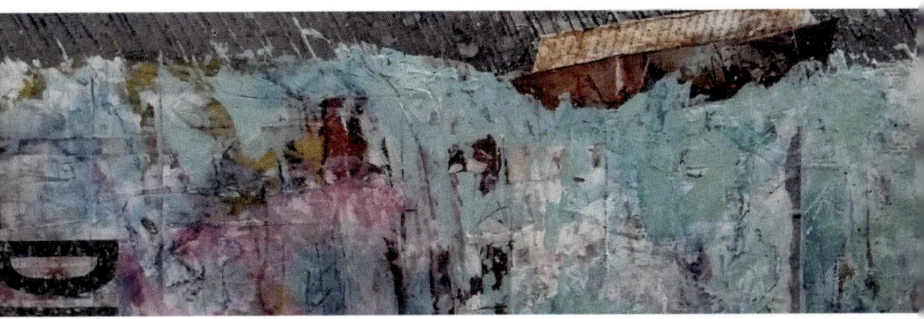

to complete one piece every day for 27 consecutive days. I wanted to consecrate each morning of Advent to paint a mixed media piece communicating that part of the genealogy and coming of Christ. It would require a few hours a day at the least, from start to completion, and working at a speed completely outside my comfort and ability. I didn't see myself adequate to the task, but I also couldn't dismiss the prompting.

The morning after Thanksgiving, I pulled out a 24"x24" canvas (the only blank one I had) and set it on the studio table. I couldn't see how I'd be able to keep this up for the full season or even finish the first day, but in place of self-confidence the Spirit supplied peace and enough faith to fill my palette with color and pick up a brush. What transpired over the next month began a surrender of my time and expectations to grow in anticipation for the next part of His story. I finished both emptied and filled on Christmas day.

In the Advent season of 2022, I dedicated my days to the same task —a new mixed media piece every day— but this time writing poetry to accompany each painting. It soon turned into a daily rhythm, a liturgy of unfolding the timeline in Scripture, planning and painting the story, then interpreting the piece through a composition of words. The endeavor proved to be challenging, but it is where I found the beauty of my Messiah again and again.

This art and poetry book is a compilation of that Advent journey and is precious to me because of the surrender it required and the awe that was ignited for the One who "declares the end from the beginning" (Isaiah 46:10). As you follow His lineage through these pages of art and poetry, I pray each day lights another candle to illuminate the marvelous story of our Wonderful Counselor, Mighty God, Everlasting Father, and Prince of Peace (Isaiah 9:6).

**The first day of this Advent journey in art and verse begins on November 29 and proceeds for twenty-seven days to December 25.*

1

IN THE BEGINNING, GOD

The light shines

in the darkness,

and the darkness

has not overcome it.

FROM SCRIPTURE, GOD TELLS HIS STORY...

GENESIS 1:1-5

In the beginning, God created the heavens and the earth. The earth was without form and void, and darkness was over the face of the deep. And the Spirit of God was hovering over the face of the waters.

And God said, "Let there be light," and there was light. And God saw that the light was good. And God separated the light from the darkness. God called the light Day, and the darkness he called Night. And there was evening and there was morning, the first day.

ISAIAH 46:9-11

"Remember the former things of old;

for I am God, and there is no other;

I am God, and there is none like me,

declaring the end from the beginning

and from ancient times things not yet done,

saying, 'My counsel shall stand,

and I will accomplish all my purpose,'

calling a bird of prey from the east,

the man of my counsel from a far country.

I have spoken, and I will bring it to pass;

I have purposed, and I will do it."

JOHN 1:1-5

In the beginning was the Word, and the Word was with God, and the Word was God. He was in the beginning with God. All things were made through him, and without him was not any thing made that was made. In him was life, and the life was the light of men. The light shines in the darkness, and the darkness has not overcome it.

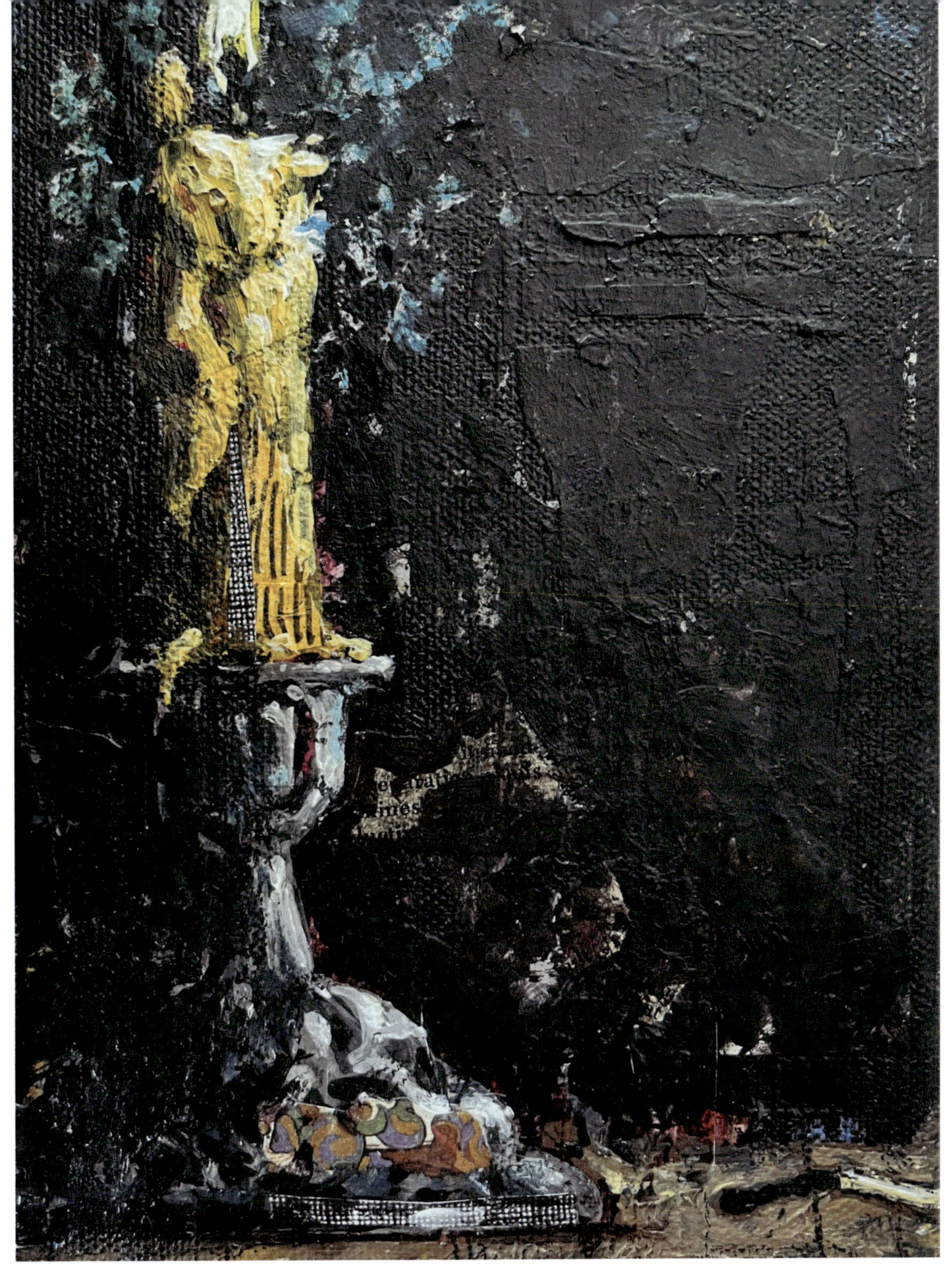

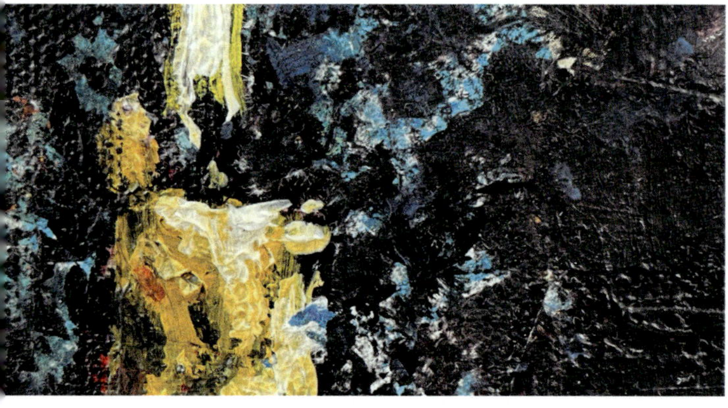

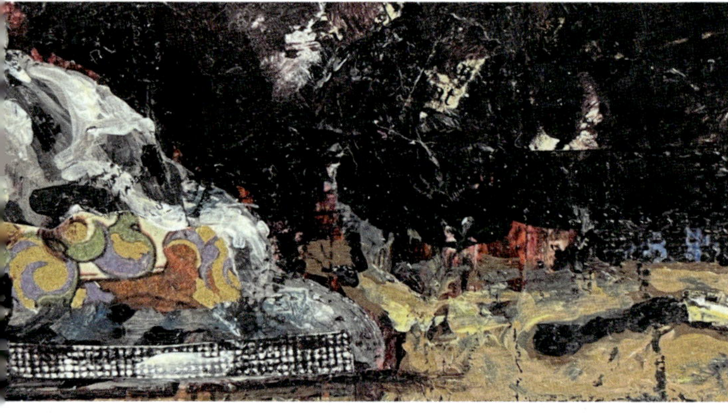

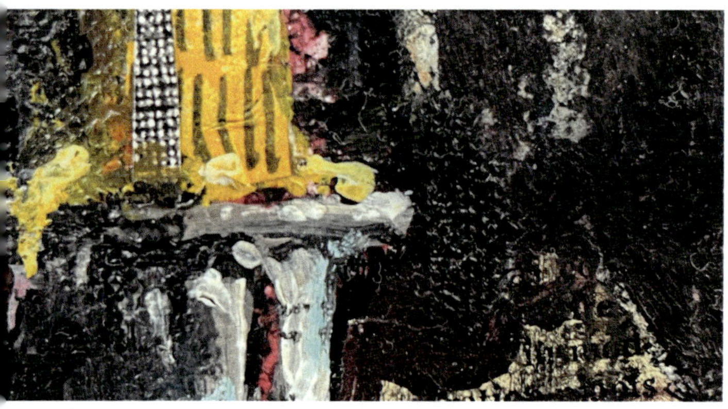

A narrative begins in the dark,
in the void a voice breaks,
"Let there be."
An artist.
A writer.
A consuming fire,
suffocating all that was shadow with light,
separating day from night,
and declaring the end
of all succeeding chapters,
from "it is good,"
to "it was made right"
here at history's flyleaf.
And still
— still —
speaking it into motion
with the notion
that Light would pierce the dark
and be pierced Himself
in kind
out of love for what he designed.
From Day One
we have shielded our eyes
from what we could not understand.
His word,
His hand,
the coming Son of Man
whose very word gave life to man.

The uncreated One
who spoke on Day One
caused dark to come undone
So that you and I,
fumbling in the dark,
could see...
Him.

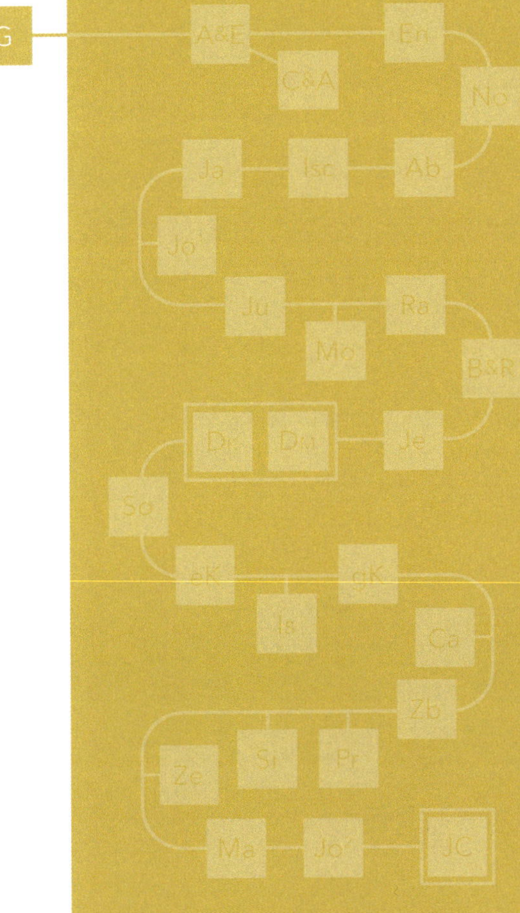

ADVENT DAY 1
IN THE BEGINNING, GOD

2

ADAM AND EVE

He shall bruise
your head,
and you shall
bruise his heel.

FROM SCRIPTURE, GOD TELLS HIS STORY...

God creates man (Genesis 2:5-9,15-17)
God creates woman (Genesis 2:18-25)

GENESIS 1:27

So God created man in his own image, in the image of God he created him; male and female he created them.

GENESIS 2:16-17

And the Lord God commanded the man, saying, "You may surely eat of every tree of the garden, but of the tree of the knowledge of good and evil you shall not eat, for in the day that you eat of it you shall surely die."

A snake in the garden (Genesis 3:1-5)
A fall in the garden (Genesis 3:6-7)

GENESIS 3:8-15

And they heard the sound of the Lord God walking in the garden in the cool of the day, and the man and his wife hid themselves from the presence of the Lord God among the trees of the garden. But the Lord God called to the man and said to him, "Where are you?" And he said, "I heard the sound of you in the garden, and I was afraid, because I was naked, and I hid myself." He said, "Who told you that you were naked? Have you eaten of the tree of which I commanded you not to eat?" The man said, "The woman whom you gave to be with me, she gave me fruit of the tree, and I ate." Then the Lord God said to the woman, "What is this that you have done?" The woman said, "The serpent deceived me, and I ate."

The Lord God said to the serpent, "Because you have done this, cursed are you above all livestock and above all beasts of the field; on your belly you shall go, and dust you shall eat all the days of your life. I will put enmity between you and the woman, and between your offspring and her offspring; he shall bruise your head, and you shall bruise his heel."

Curses and a covering (Genesis 3:16-21)

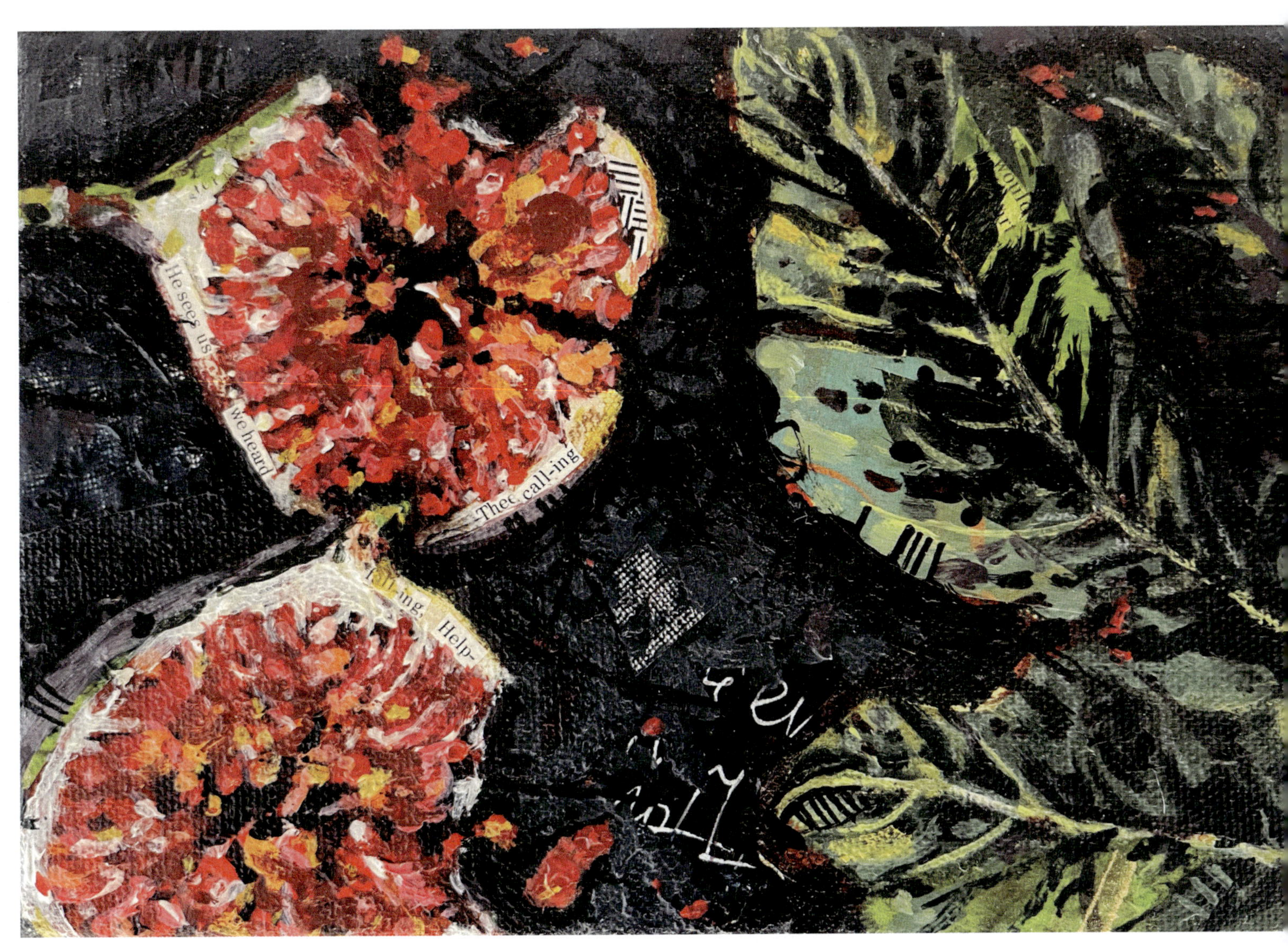
He sees us
we heard
Thee call-ing
Help-

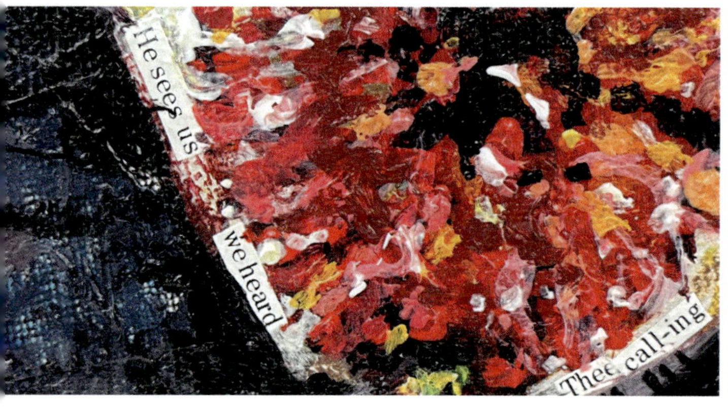

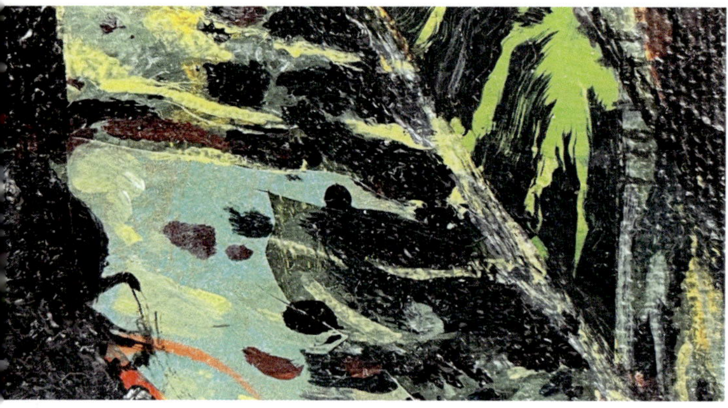

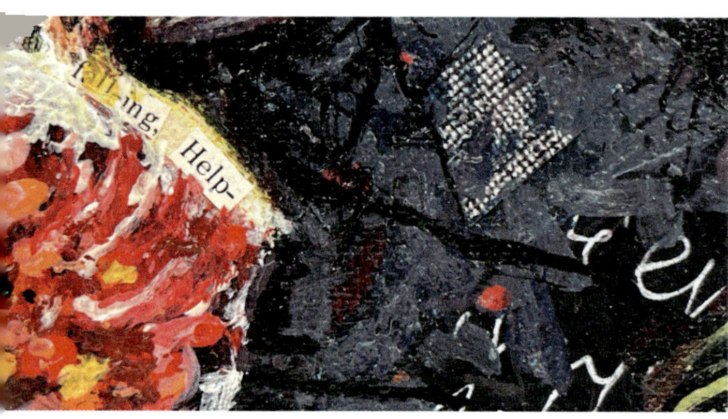

A man.
A woman.
A good design.
Image of the divine.
Image.
What they needed, they were given
in this garden in Eden.
The Maker still had his reason
for planting
one special tree.
Its knowledge set apart
for the One who could bear it...
the One who made it,
not those he created.
Taking the fruit was a sin.
It didn't belong to them.
But the serpent stepped in.
"Did God really say?" he began,
and she leaned in
to hear a different tune.
And the Piper's song was sweet,
as was the fruit.
They could replace the Giver
if they just tried.
Surely
they would not die.
Try...
and see.

And eyes were opened.
"It is good" was broken.
It was true what was spoken.
Just like He said.
Hiding and hearing
the Maker was nearing.
They answered,
all covered in Fall leaves.
Fall curses.
Fall blame.
Fall serpent.
Fall shame.
Fall grace as the Maker
tells the end.
A bruise.
A blow.
Another seed would grow
to cover all we owed
from now to then.

We wait on Him.

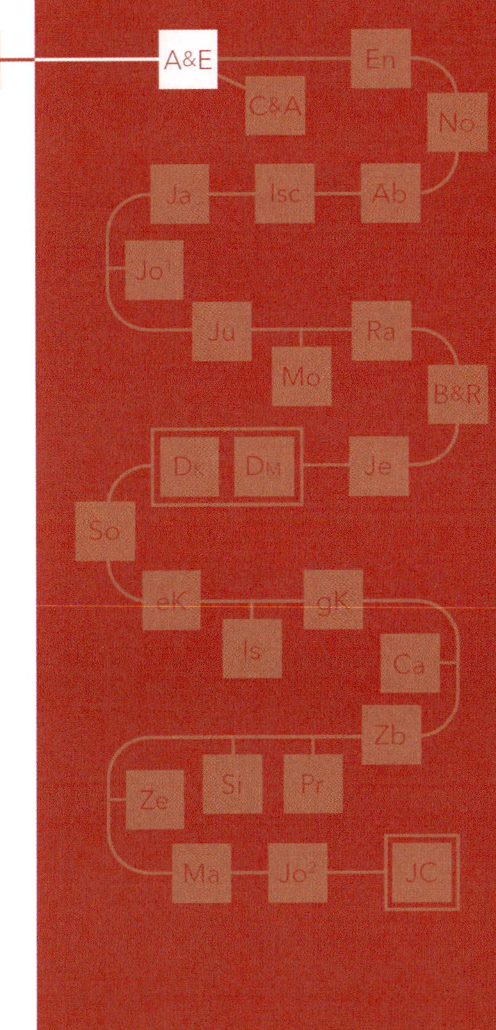

ADVENT DAY 2
ADAM AND EVE

3

CAIN AND ABEL, ENOCH

Without faith it is impossible to please Him.

FROM SCRIPTURE, GOD TELLS HIS STORY...

GENESIS 4:3-12,16

In the course of time Cain brought to the Lord an offering of the fruit of the ground, and Abel also brought of the firstborn of his flock and of their fat portions. And the Lord had regard for Abel and his offering, but for Cain and his offering he had no regard.
So Cain was very angry, and his face fell. The Lord said to Cain, "Why are you angry, and why has your face fallen? If you do well, will you not be accepted? And if you do not do well, sin is crouching at the door. Its desire is contrary to you, but you must rule over it."

Cain spoke to Abel his brother. And when they were in the field, Cain rose up against his brother Abel and killed him. Then the Lord said to Cain, "Where is Abel your brother?" He said, "I do not know; am I my brother's keeper?" And the Lord said, "What have you done? The voice of your brother's blood is crying to me from the ground. And now you are cursed from the ground, which has opened its mouth to receive your brother's blood from your hand. When you work the ground, it shall no longer yield to you its strength. You shall be a fugitive and a wanderer on the earth."

...Then Cain went away from the presence of the Lord and settled in the land of Nod, east of Eden.

GENESIS 5:22-24

Enoch walked with God after he fathered Methuselah 300 years and had other sons and daughters. Thus all the days of Enoch were 365 years. Enoch walked with God, and he was not, for God took him.

HEBREWS 11:5-6

By faith Enoch was taken up so that he should not see death, and he was not found, because God had taken him. Now before he was taken he was commended as having pleased God. And without faith it is impossible to please him, for whoever would draw near to God must believe that he exists and that he rewards those who seek him.

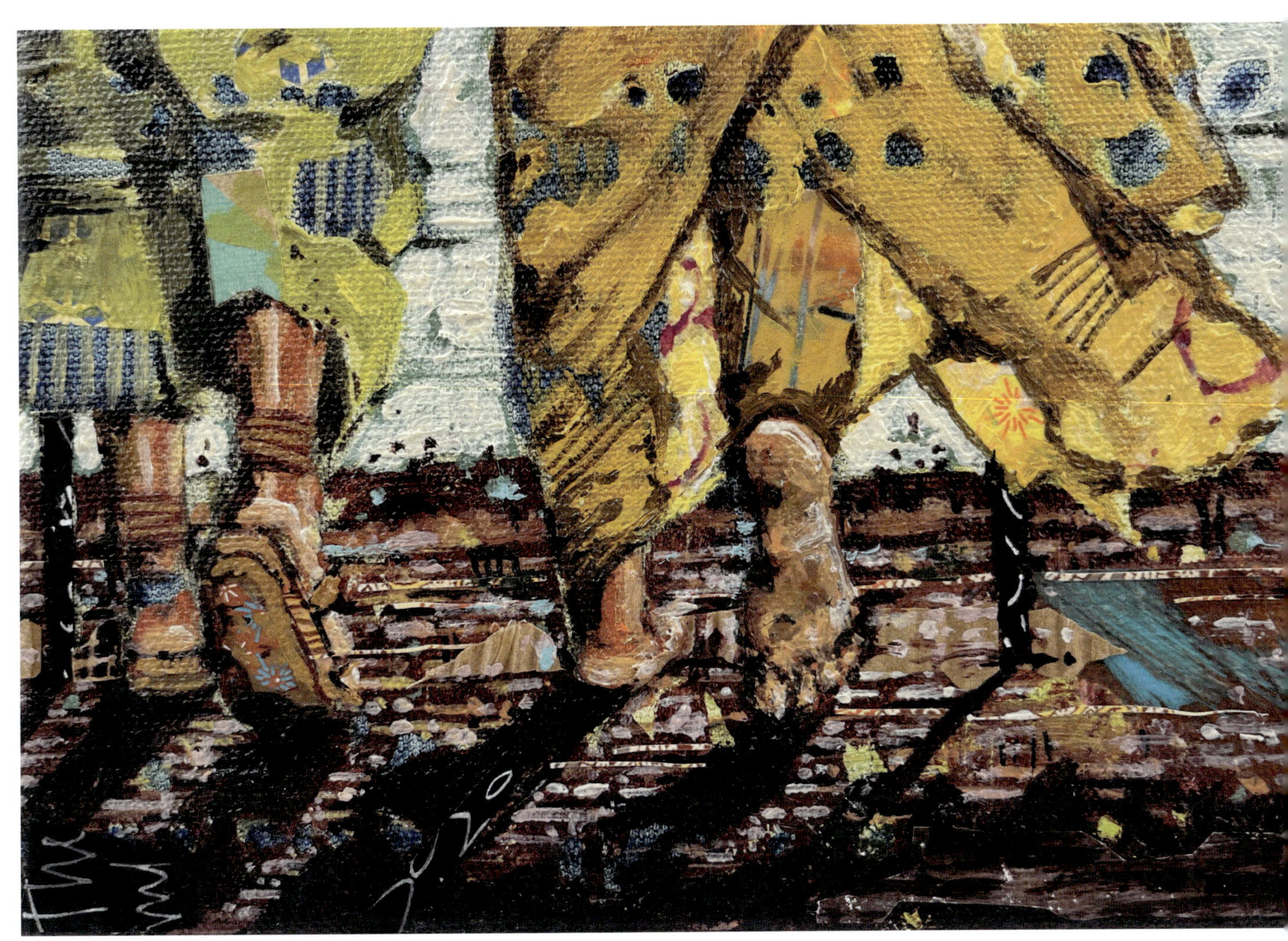

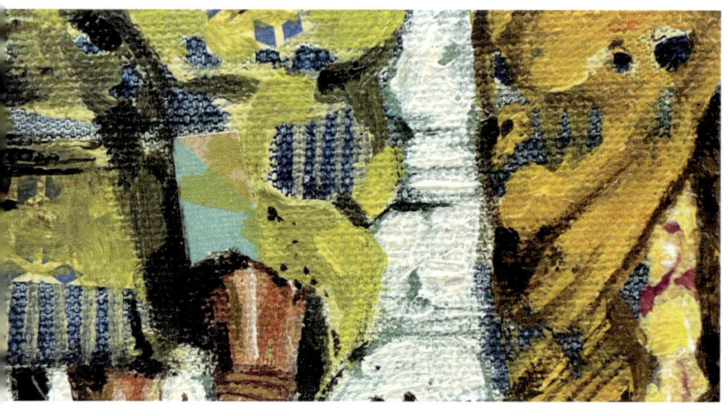

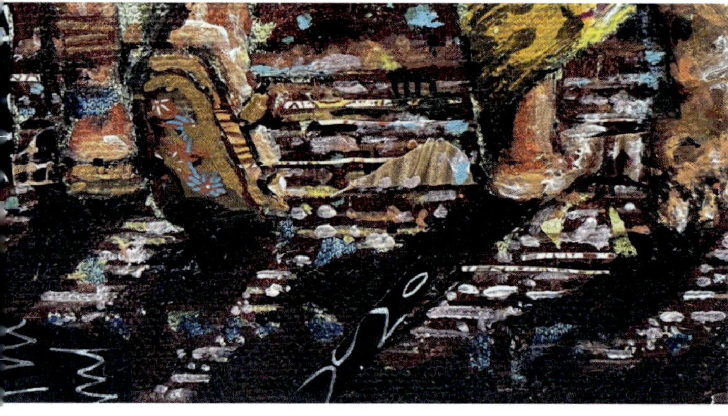

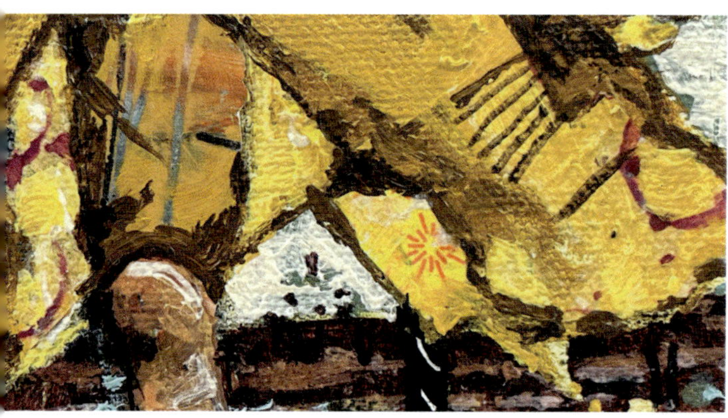

Adam and Eve,
covered by a life taken,
the cost now draping
across their shoulders to bear in mind.
A Seed to find down the line
— their line.
Posterity offered the hope God vowed.
They bore fruit in time,
after their kind.
Two brothers.
Post garden,
post fall.
Enmity took root
and fear strangled all rest;
Everything a test of "Did God really say?"
Knowledge of a right and wrong way.
But an offering
— a sacrifice of what was made —
would honor the cost paid.
So Abel prepared,
to the Father's delight,
what was right
and in step to what
and Who he knew.
But just as Cain expected,
his portion was rejected
because he knew what to do
and refused.

His own way Cain would choose.
In anger then,
more sin upon sin,
Cain offered a blow;
took Abel's life instead.
With hands stained red,
the wandering Cain
fled.

But Enoch,
seven generations down that same line,
in a world of Cain's kind,
would live not by sight,
but by faith.
Constant walks,
childlike talks,
until his pace was in stride
with his Father's.
Never saw death
with his final breath.
Just finished the walk they started.

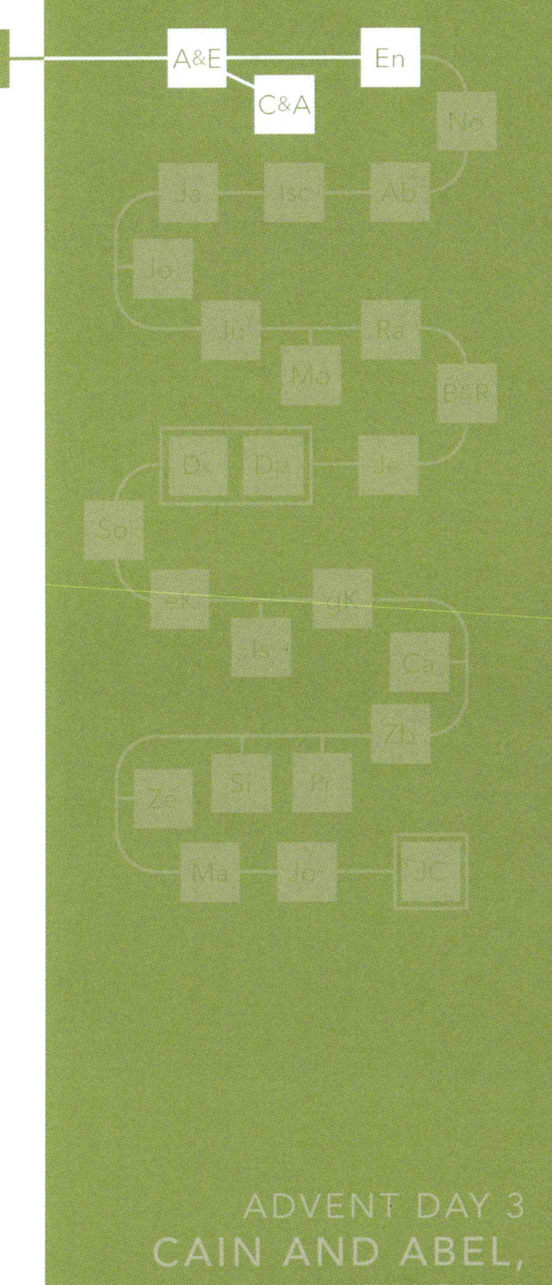

ADVENT DAY 3

CAIN AND ABEL, ENOCH

4

NOAH

In the days of Noah,
eight people
were brought safely
through the water.

FROM SCRIPTURE, GOD TELLS HIS STORY...

GENESIS 6:5,7-8,11-14

The Lord saw that the wickedness of man was great in the earth, and that every intention of the thoughts of his heart was only evil continually ... So the Lord said, "I will blot out man whom I have created from the face of the land, man and animals and creeping things and birds of the heavens, for I am sorry that I have made them." But Noah found favor in the eyes of the Lord.

...Now the earth was corrupt in God's sight, and the earth was filled with violence. And God saw the earth, and behold, it was corrupt, for all flesh had corrupted their way on the earth. And God said to Noah, "I have determined to make an end of all flesh, for the earth is filled with violence through them. Behold, I will destroy them with the earth. Make yourself an ark.

Instructions (Genesis 6:14-7:4)

GENESIS 7:5

And Noah did all that the Lord had commanded him.

The flood and the ark (Genesis 7:6-24)

GENESIS 8:11

And the dove came back to him in the evening, and behold, in her mouth was a freshly plucked olive leaf. So Noah knew that the waters had subsided from the earth.

The waters cease (Genesis 8:1-19)
God's promise (Genesis 8:20-22; 9:8-17)

HEBREWS 11:7

By faith Noah, being warned by God concerning events as yet unseen, in reverent fear constructed an ark for the saving of his household. By this he condemned the world and became an heir of the righteousness that comes by faith.

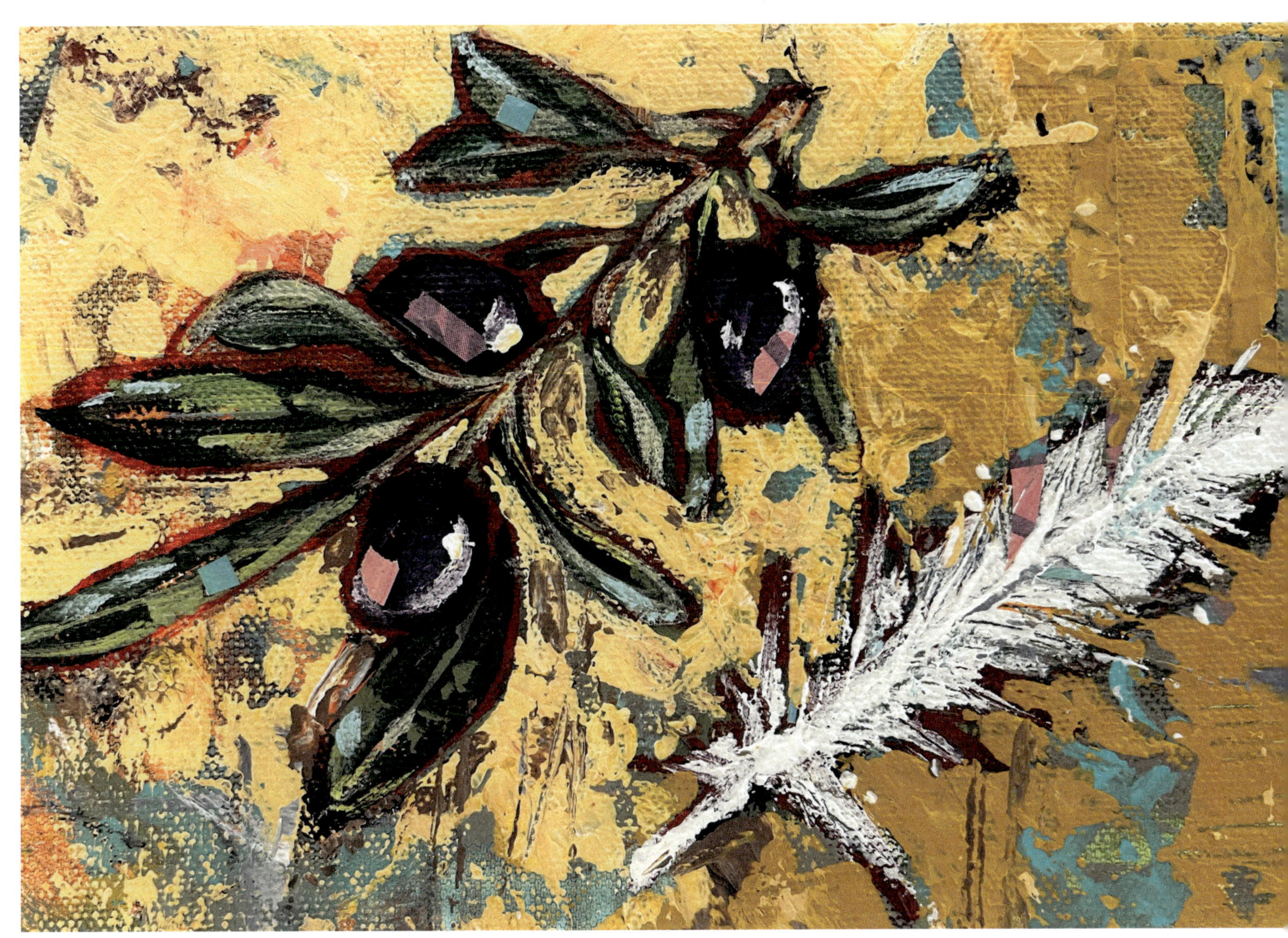

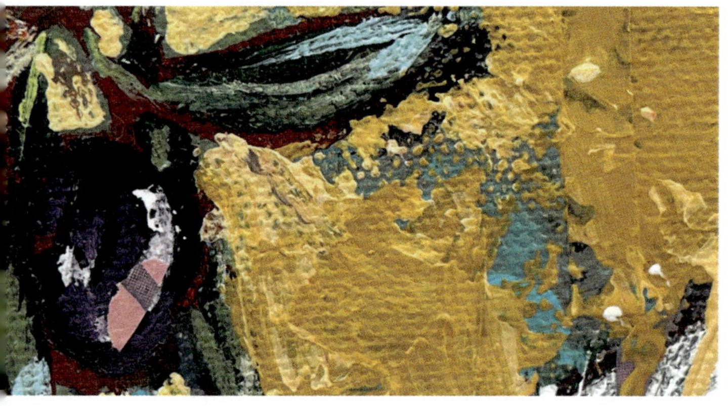

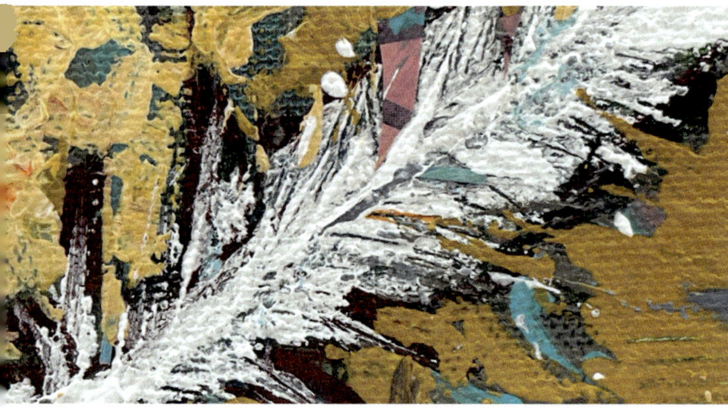

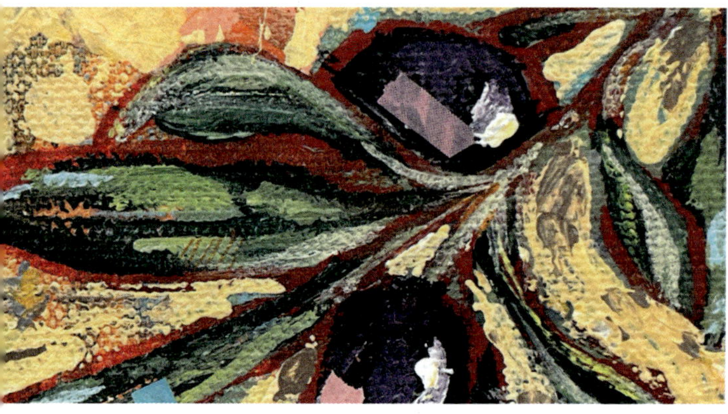

The world
living day after day
off God's grace,
then cursing his face
and still seeing
no trace of rain.
"You alone," God had said.
Because in stark contrast to the rest,
Noah would not test
the goodness of God,
but understood both
the weight of the curse
and the favor he did not deserve.
He kept close to the One
who would cover and carry.
So Noah held a hammer
and a light;
built a boat day and night.
Seemed in vain.
There was no rain.
But he trusted what God said.
On the day it was finished,
the creatures went in it
followed closely by Noah's family, too.
The door,
God closed it.
The sin,
He exposed it.

And wrath fell like rain that day.
Those within
were covered and carried,
while those without
were caught and buried
in a flood
they said would never come.
Awful and amazing
— God's judgment and saving.
For 40 days He kept them.
Kept His covenant too.
It was all made new.
"What was" was dead.
They looked ahead
to a new creation.
So when the waters abated,
they faithfully waited
for a sign.
And the dove returned
with a love letter.
Peace.

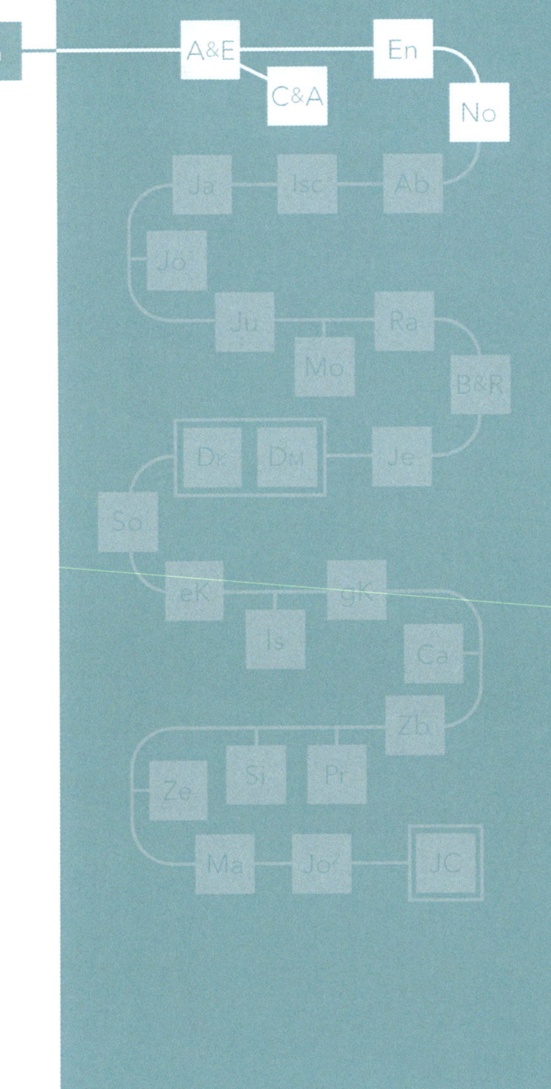

ADVENT DAY 4
NOAH

5

ABRAHAM

He went out,

not knowing

where he was going.

FROM SCRIPTURE, GOD TELLS HIS STORY...

GENESIS 12:1-4

Now the Lord said to Abram, "Go from your country and your kindred and your father's house to the land that I will show you. And I will make of you a great nation, and I will bless you and make your name great, so that you will be a blessing. I will bless those who bless you, and him who dishonors you I will curse, and in you all the families of the earth shall be blessed."

So Abram went, as the Lord had told him...

Fear, famine, and fighting (Genesis 12-13)
Saving Lot (Genesis 14)
Counting stars and a covenant (Genesis 15)

GENESIS 15:6

And he believed the Lord, and he counted it to him as righteousness.

Schemes (Genesis 16)
New names (Genesis 17)
Visitors (Genesis 18)
Lies, again (Genesis 20)
A promised son and a test (Genesis 21-22)

HEBREWS 11:8-12

By faith Abraham obeyed when he was called to go out to a place that he was to receive as an inheritance. And he went out, not knowing where he was going.
By faith he went to live in the land of promise, as in a foreign land, living in tents with Isaac and Jacob, heirs with him of the same promise. For he was looking forward to the city that has foundations, whose designer and builder is God.
By faith Sarah herself received power to conceive, even when she was past the age, since she considered him faithful who had promised. Therefore from one man, and him as good as dead, were born descendants as many as the stars of heaven and as many as the innumerable grains of sand by the seashore.

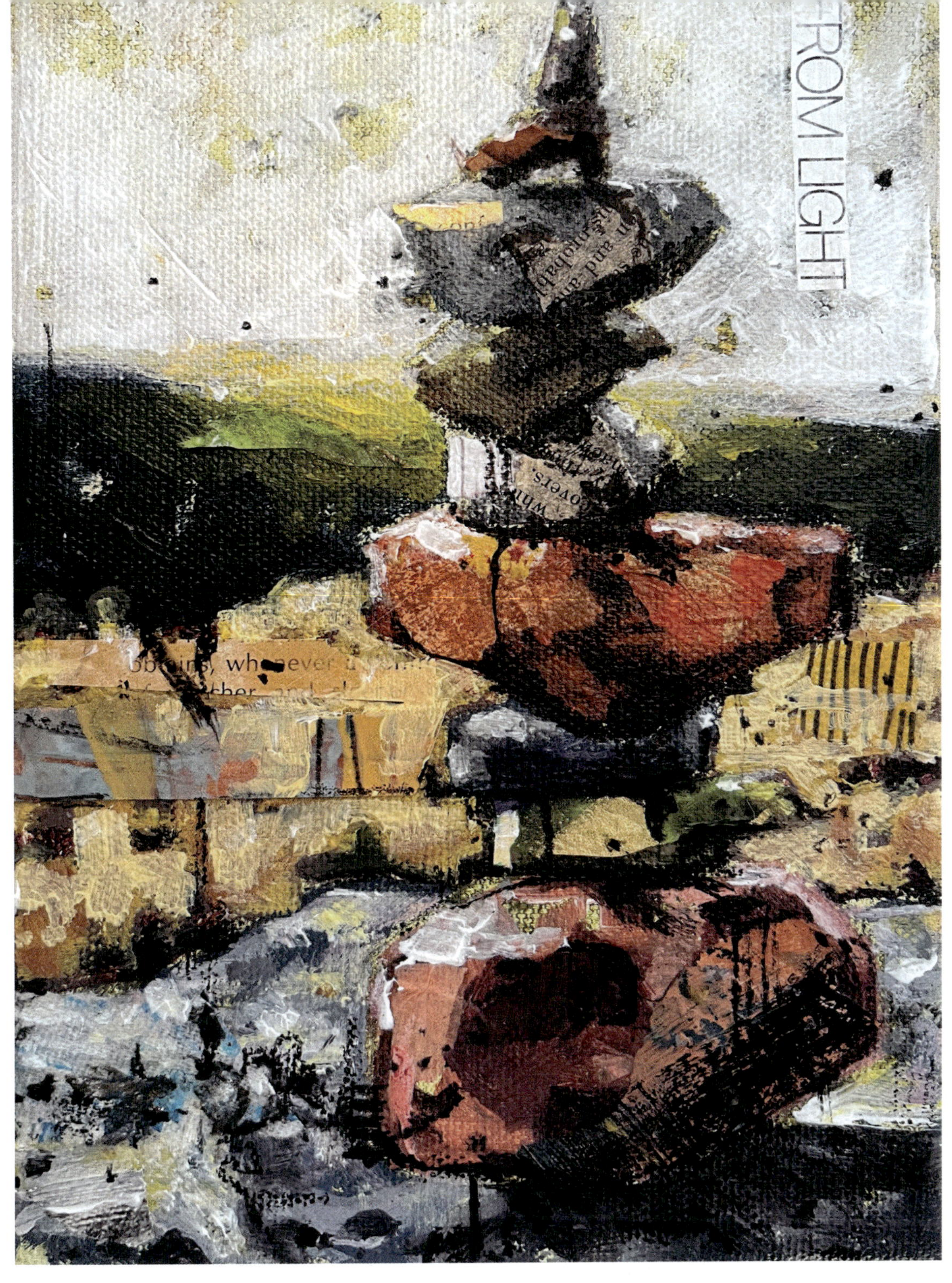
FROM LIGHT

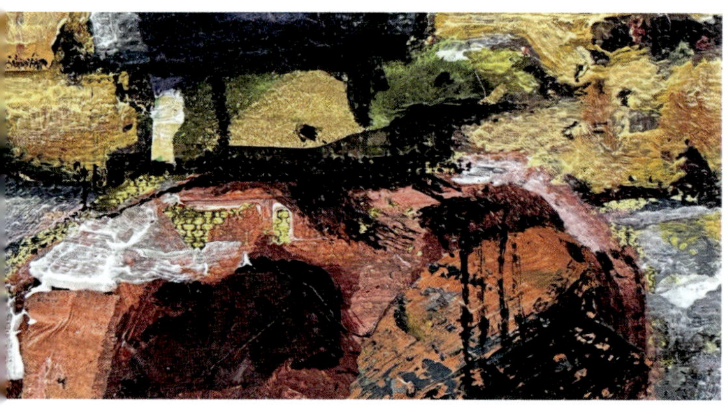

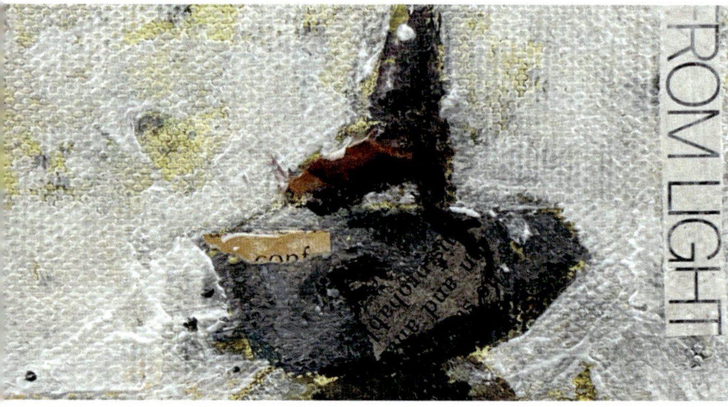

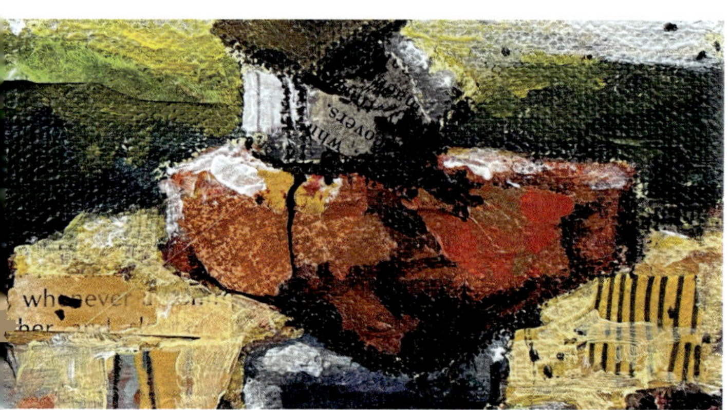

We say we want adventure
but gravity pulls us to a plan,
a place we can land,
a routine we demand.
We believe it saves us
— the safe familiar —
but will it ever break us of ourselves?
We won't change unless we are compelled.
Abram had roots too until God called.
"Pack it up.
Leave it all and go
to the place where I will show."
The promise was compelling,
fortelling a dwelling,
his name and family line,
blessing all mankind.
A sojourn with God as the guide.
Fear inside, but compelled to believe.
Next home, unknown.

A journey of trial and error.
Affirmation followed terror
on one particular night
after a fight and
overcome with fright.
God pointed out the stars
and quieted his trembling heart.
"I will never part from my vow.

Though you don't know how,
I do."
Abraham still standing still,
wide-eyed, listening,
not wishing, but believing.

Cairns marked where he'd been.
Here he lied.
Here he gave up.
Here he cried.
Here he took back.
Every place where he was taken
was a point where he was shaken
to filter fear and replace it with belief.
Here he bypassed.
Here he carried.
Here he bargained.
Here he buried.
A sojourn that made much of Another.
Looking back he saw
a well-worn path
to his Father.
His roots were in a Person,
not a place.
The father of many
lived by faith.

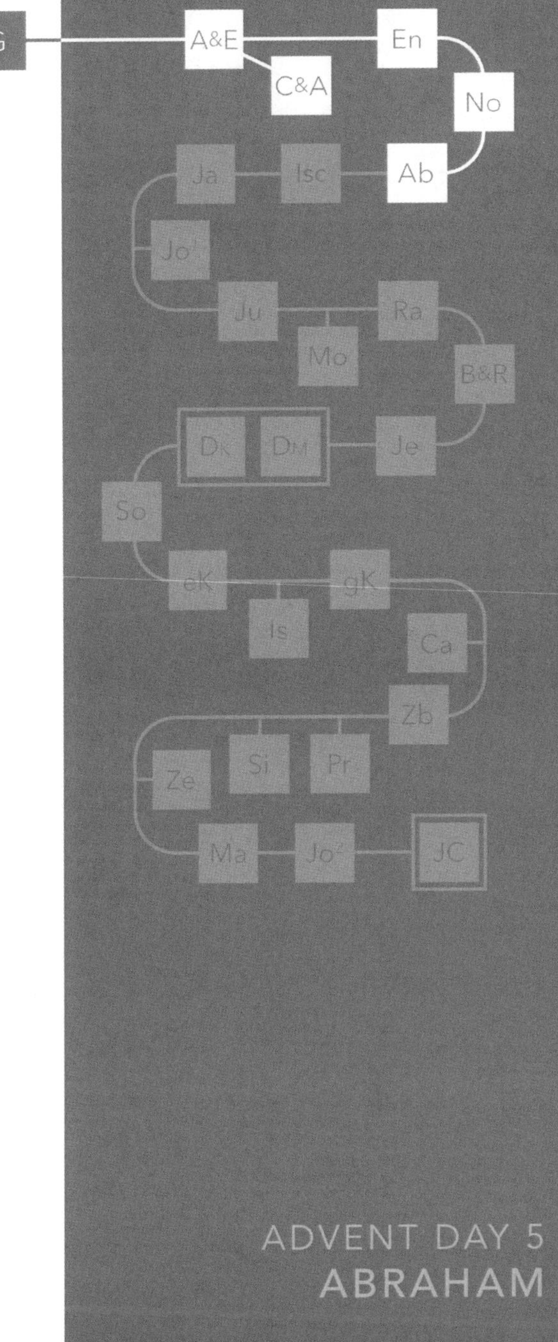

ADVENT DAY 5
ABRAHAM

6
ISAAC

On the mount

of the Lord

it shall be provided.

FROM SCRIPTURE, GOD TELLS HIS STORY...

Isaac is born (Genesis 21:1-7)

GENESIS 22:1-14

After these things God tested Abraham and said to him, "Abraham!" And he said, "Here I am." He said, "Take your son, your only son Isaac, whom you love, and go to the land of Moriah, and offer him there as a burnt offering on one of the mountains of which I shall tell you." So Abraham rose early in the morning, saddled his donkey, and took two of his young men with him, and his son Isaac. And he cut the wood for the burnt offering and arose and went to the place of which God had told him. On the third day Abraham lifted up his eyes and saw the place from afar. ... And Abraham took the wood of the burnt offering and laid it on Isaac his son. And he took in his hand the fire and the knife. So they went both of them together. And Isaac said to his father Abraham, "My father!" And he said, "Here I am, my son." He said, "Behold, the fire and the wood, but where is the lamb for a burnt offering?" Abraham said, "God will provide for himself the lamb for a burnt offering, my son." So they went both of them together.

When they came to the place of which God had told him, Abraham built the altar there and laid the wood in order and bound Isaac his son and laid him on the altar, on top of the wood. Then Abraham reached out his hand and took the knife to slaughter his son. But the angel of the LORD called to him from heaven and said, "Abraham, Abraham!" And he said, "Here I am." He said, "Do not lay your hand on the boy or do anything to him, for now I know that you fear God, seeing you have not withheld your son, your only son, from me." And Abraham lifted up his eyes and looked, and behold, behind him was a ram, caught in a thicket by his horns. And Abraham went and took the ram and offered it up as a burnt offering instead of his son. So Abraham called the name of that place, "The LORD will provide."

A declaration (Genesis 22:16-18)
The foretold sacrifice of another beloved Son (Isaiah 53)

HEBREWS 11:17-19

By faith Abraham, when he was tested, offered up Isaac, and he who had received the promises was in the act of offering up his only son, of whom it was said, "Through Isaac shall your offspring be named." He considered that God was able even to raise him from the dead, from which, figuratively speaking, he did receive him back.

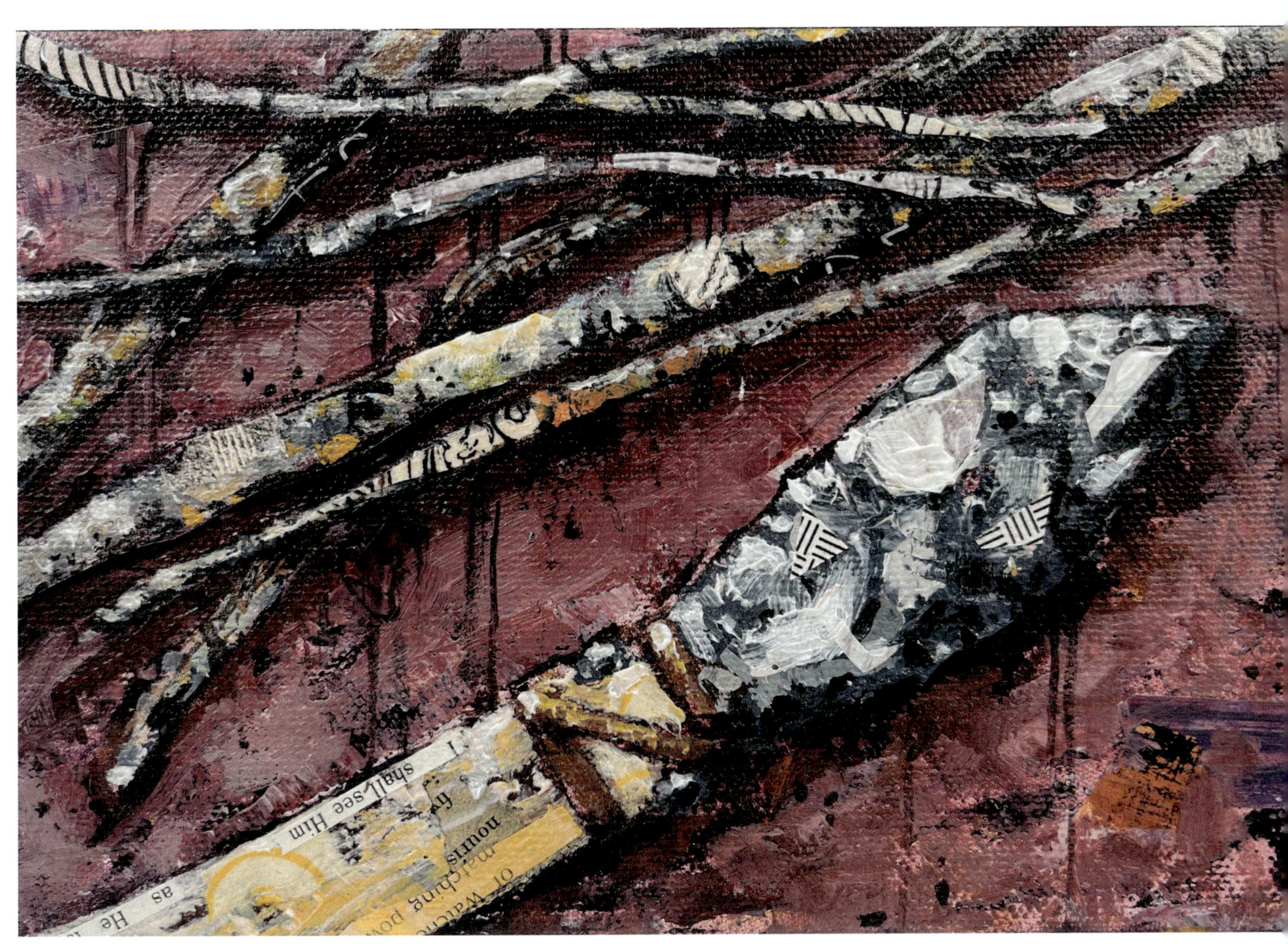
I
shall see Him

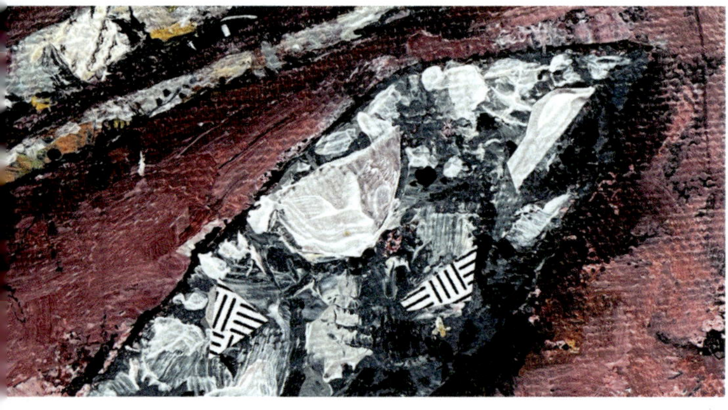

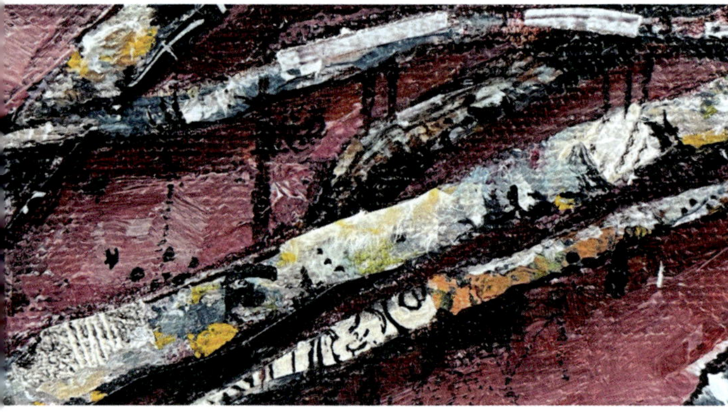

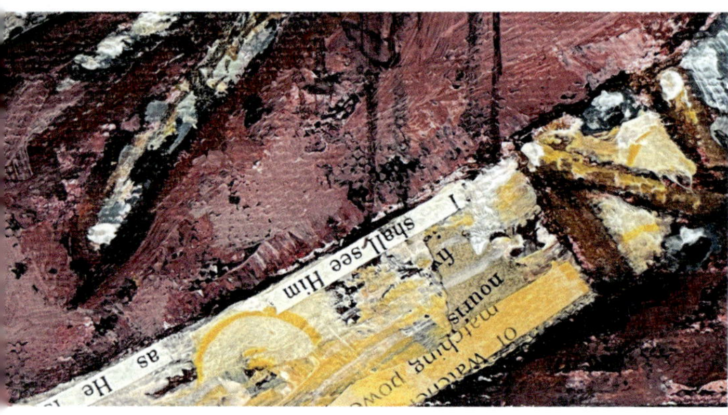

A peculiar friend God had been to Abraham
but faithful in every way.
Like that day when God gave he and Sarah a son,
the only begotten, promised one.
Isaac grew.
Abraham's love too.
The promise of God now rested on him.
(These were the very words
of his faithful Friend.)
But then
a strange ask,
a required task.
"Take your son,
your one and only,
place him on an altar.
Offer up his life to me."
Confusion ensued.
But Abraham knew
God didn't lie, tease, or ask such a task
with meaningless ease.
Departing at dawn
with Isaac, his son.
Three days to deliberate while carefully answering
Isaac's *whys, hows,* and *how much farther nows.*
"We have the wood and flame,
but where is the lamb to be slain?"
What was he to say?
"God will provide today."

Up a hill
until they stood still.
Not a sound as the altar was made,
then the father laid his son down.
And as he released his grip on what he didn't understand,
he tightened the one on the knife
to take the life of the one he'd been given.
At the point of total surrender,
God would render him right.
Faith was made sight.
His hand would be stopped
and a ram caught nearby to take his place.
A saving grace.

One day this same scene would play again.
To please the Father.
The beloved, begotten son
— the only one —
would carry wood up a hill for our sin.
But noone would stop death's hand.
And God would provide
again.

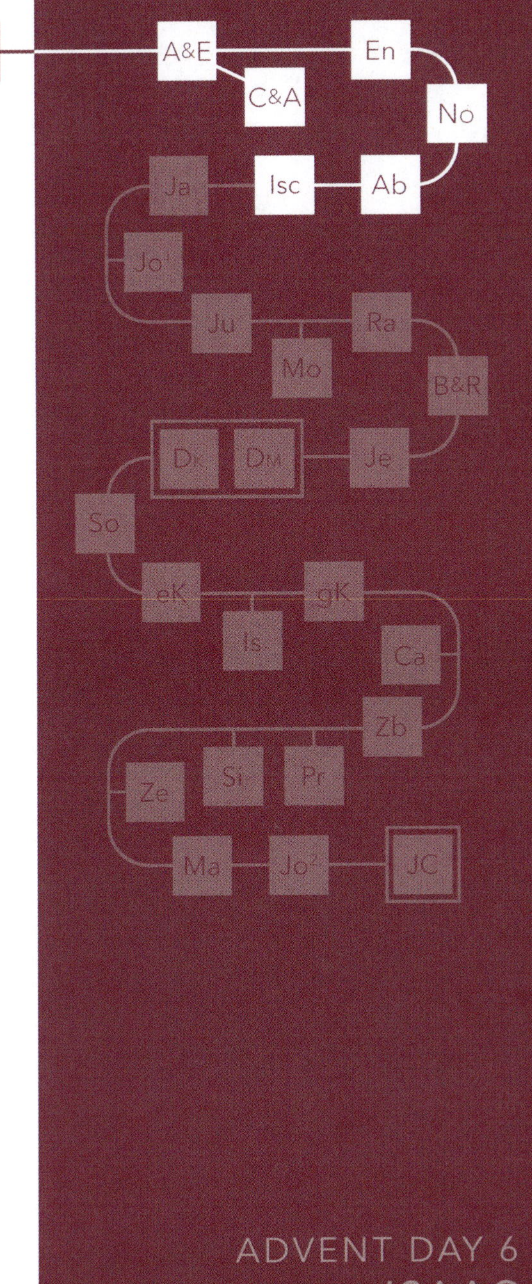

ADVENT DAY 6

ISAAC

7

JACOB

Surely the Lord is in this place and I was unaware of it.

FROM SCRIPTURE, GOD TELLS HIS STORY...

GENESIS 25:21-26

And Isaac prayed to the Lord for his wife, because she was barren. And the Lord granted his prayer, and Rebekah his wife conceived. The children struggled together within her, and she said, "If it is thus, why is this happening to me?" So she went to inquire of the Lord. And the Lord said to her,

"Two nations are in your womb, and two peoples from within you shall be divided; the one shall be stronger than the other, the older shall serve the younger."

When her days to give birth were completed, behold, there were twins in her womb. The first came out red, all his body like a hairy cloak, so they called his name Esau. Afterward his brother came out with his hand holding Esau's heel, so his name was called Jacob. Isaac was sixty years old when she bore them.

An exchange (Genesis 25:27-34)
The plan and aftermath (Genesis 27:1-28:5)
A dream (Genesis 28:10-22)
Another exchange (Genesis 29:1-30)
A dozen (Genesis 29:31-30:25; 35:16-20,22-27)
Returning home (Genesis 31:1-7,13-18; 32:1-33:16; 35:27-29)

GENESIS 32:24-30

And Jacob was left alone. And a man wrestled with him until the breaking of the day. When the man saw that he did not prevail against Jacob, he touched his hip socket, and Jacob's hip was put out of joint as he wrestled with him. Then he said, "Let me go, for the day has broken." But Jacob said, "I will not let you go unless you bless me." And he said to him, "What is your name?" And he said, "Jacob." Then he said, "Your name shall no longer be called Jacob, but Israel, for you have striven with God and with men, and have prevailed." Then Jacob asked him, "Please tell me your name." But he said, "Why is it that you ask my name?" And there he blessed him. So Jacob called the name of the place Peniel, saying, "For I have seen God face to face, and yet my life has been delivered."

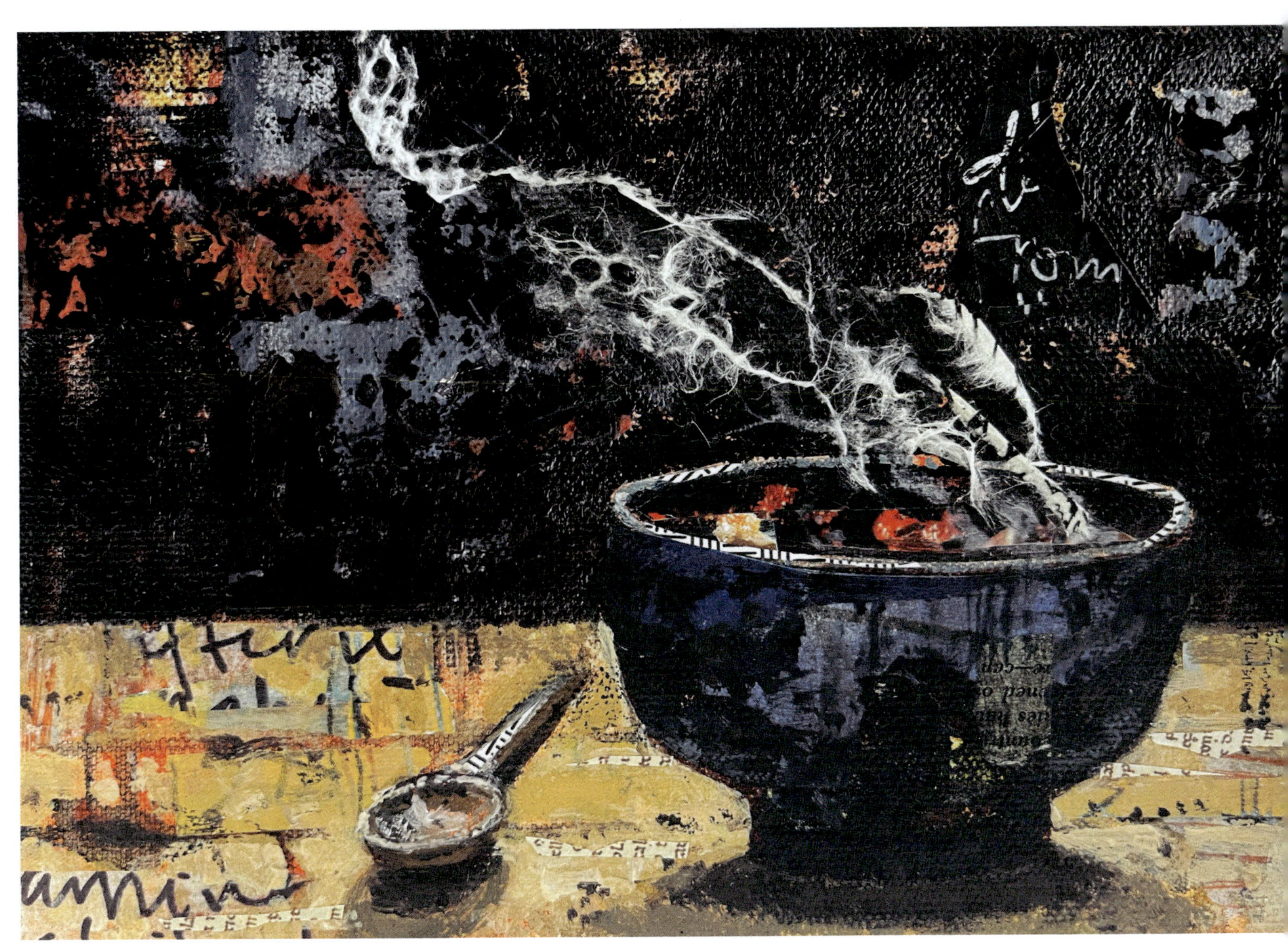

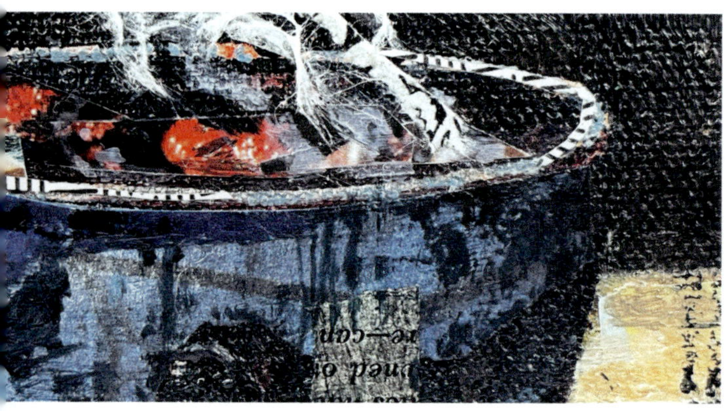

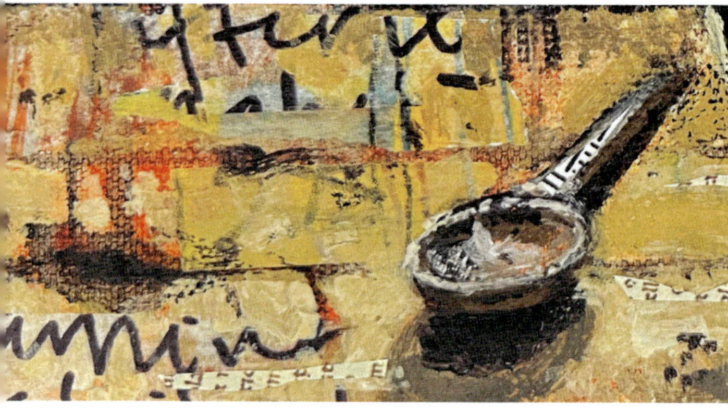

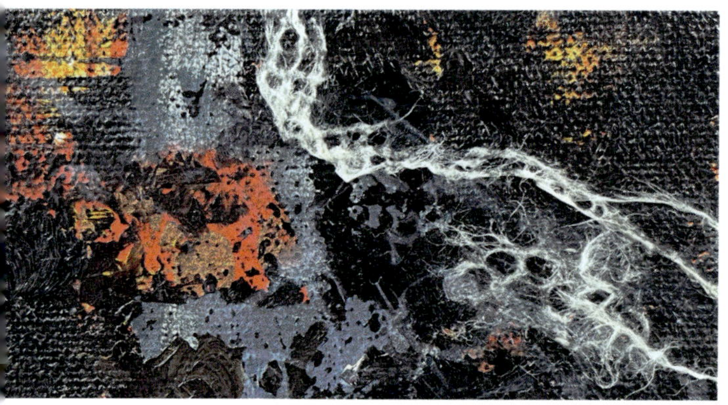

Isaac, now a man,
took Rebekah's hand and prayed for an heir.
Twins, to their delight,
but Esau and Jacob would fight
from the womb.
Between the two brothers
one would supplant the other
twice,
over a bowl of stew.
The birthright in lieu
(feeding one who was sighing),
the blessing in view
(from the one who was dying),
now extended to the younger of the two
— Jacob.
Esau hated and planned to kill
the one who would steal
what he had carelessly given away.
Jacob did not stay
but fled in fear.
Surely God was not near him here.
Compass askew.

That night, a dream.
The Lord, it would seem.
"I'm the friend of your father,
his father too.
All the land in view belongs to you
I have chosen."

Shaken awake,
he would take a stone and mark the place.

Years after his family grew,
possessions too,
he would return to meet the brother he supplanted.
Childhood home in sight,
he would pause one night
to fight the battle and fear within.
Instead
he fought with another
until the break of day.
His hip would pay,
but Jacob refused to give way
until blessed.
This was his test.
Wrestling both God and man,
a new life began,
one with promise, a limp, and new name
— Israel.
Father of twelve sons
whose lives would be undone
and woven into another Son coming.
More blessing and testing,
regrets and confessing
would yet stew in this family tree.

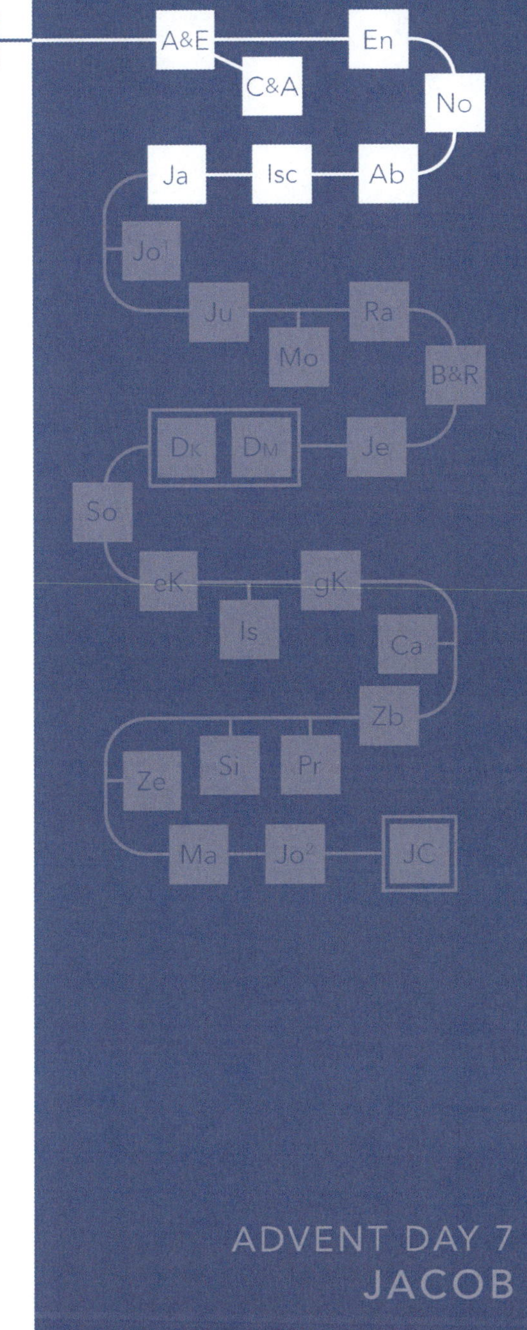

ADVENT DAY 7
JACOB

8

JOSEPH, SON OF JACOB

You meant evil

against me,

but God

meant it for good.

FROM SCRIPTURE, GOD TELLS HIS STORY...

GENESIS 37:1-5

Joseph, being seventeen years old, was pasturing the flock with his brothers … And Joseph brought a bad report of them to their father. Now Israel loved Joseph more than any other of his sons, because he was the son of his old age. And he made him a robe of many colors. But when his brothers saw that their father loved him more than all his brothers, they hated him and could not speak peacefully to him.

Now Joseph had a dream, and when he told it to his brothers they hated him even more.

The dreamer (Genesis 37:6-11)
The brothers' plan (Genesis 37:12-35)

GENESIS 37:23-24

When Joseph came to his brothers, they stripped him of his robe, the robe of many colors that he wore. And they took him and threw him into a pit.

The slave in Egypt (Genesis 37:36; 39:1-23)
The slave interprets dreams (Genesis 40:1-41:38)
The slave is elevated (Genesis 41:39-57)
The governor meets the brothers (Genesis 42:1-44:34)

GENESIS 45:1-5

Then Joseph could not control himself before all those who stood by him. He cried, "Make everyone go out from me." So no one stayed with him when Joseph made himself known to his brothers. And he wept aloud, so that the Egyptians heard it, and the household of Pharaoh heard it. And Joseph said to his brothers, "I am Joseph! Is my father still alive?" But his brothers could not answer him, for they were dismayed at his presence.

So Joseph said to his brothers, "Come near to me, please." And they came near. And he said, "I am your brother, Joseph, whom you sold into Egypt. And now do not be distressed or angry with yourselves because you sold me here, for God sent me before you to preserve life.

The King provides (Genesis 45:6-47:12)

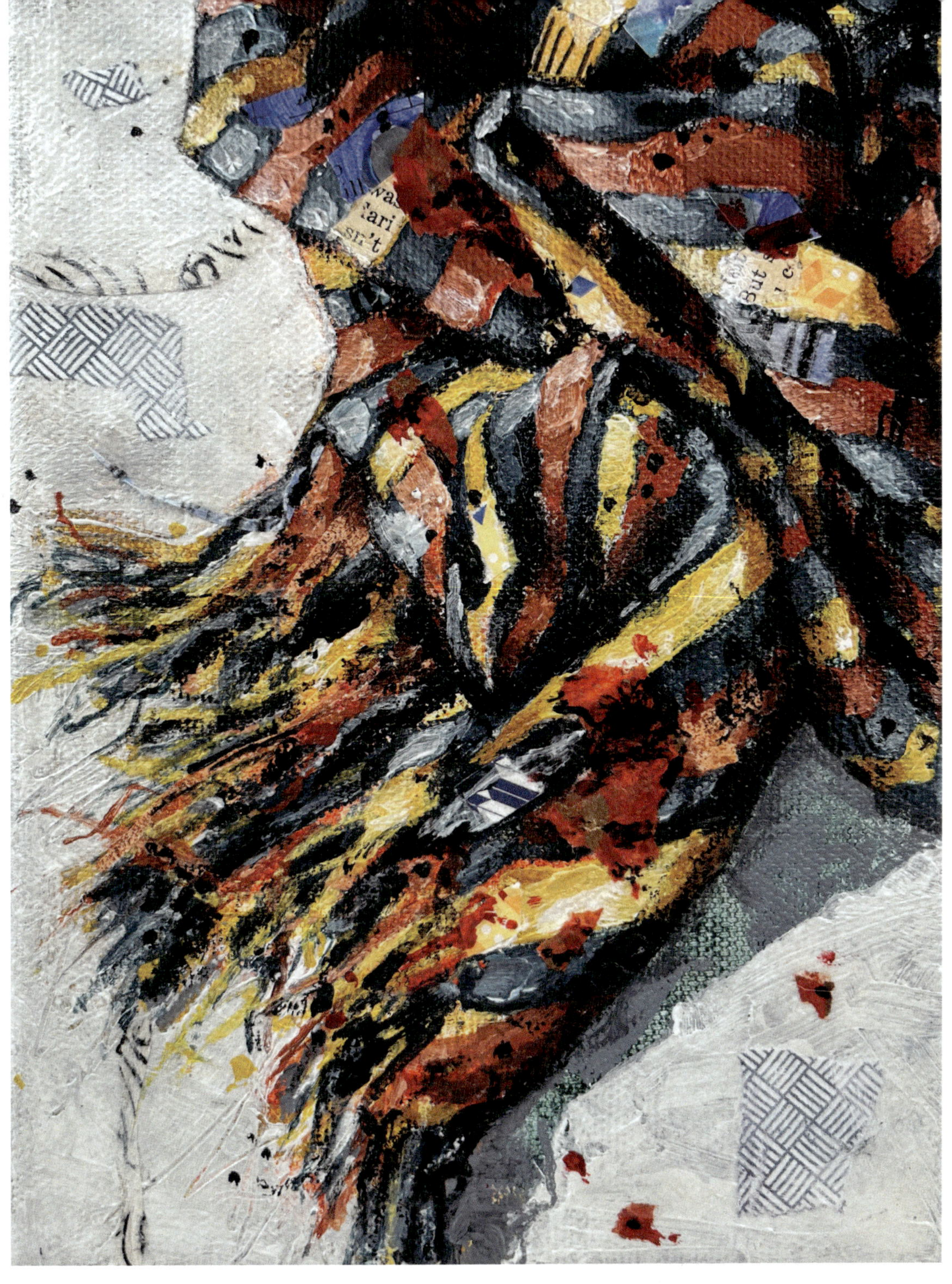

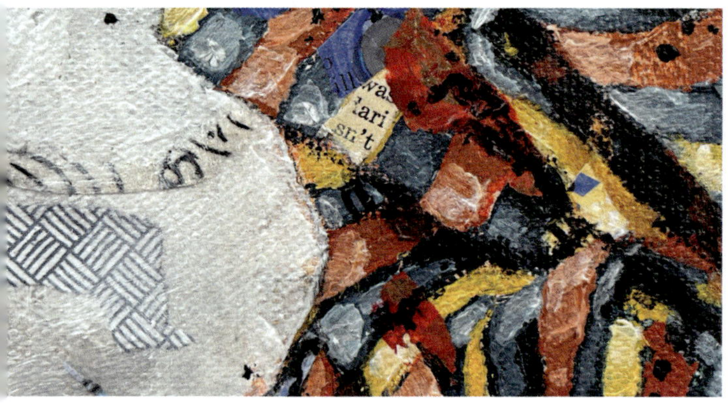

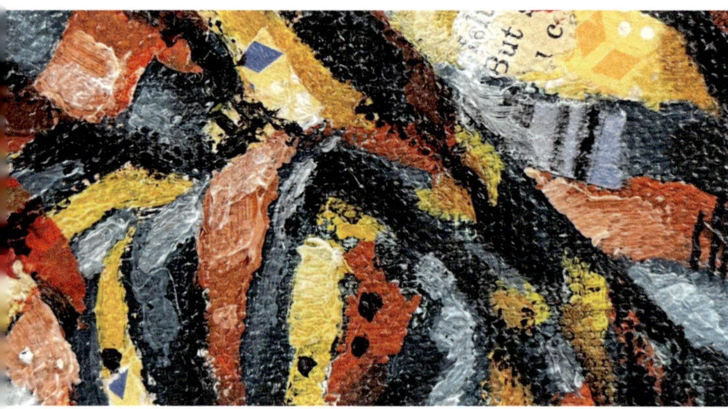

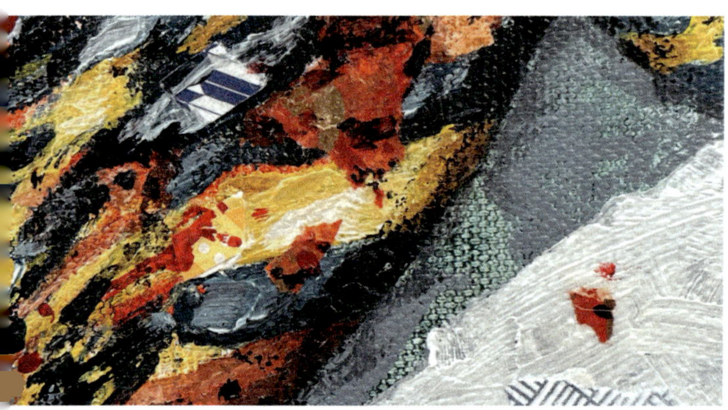

Of all his sons,
Israel loved Joseph most
and jealousy arose.
Unlike his brothers,
Joseph wore a robe of colors
his father had made.
He was quick to relay his dreams too,
how 11 sheaves in the field
and 11 stars in the night
would all bow
to him.
So they plotted to kill the Dreamer
until Reuben stepped in.
They unrobed him and sold him
to Egypt-bound traders.
Traitors. Haters.
Placed the blood-stained robe
in their father's hands
and lied;
said he died,
attacked like prey.
Israel went into mourning that day.
And Joseph, assumed dead, was a slave instead
to a man who served Egypt's king.
Favored in the eyes of his master,
by his wife too,
an advancement turned disaster.
A lie covered his robe again
landing him this time in prison.

But Joseph could dream,
a gift it seemed.
Moved him from shackles to second in command.
He gave Pharaoh a plan.
Egypt would strive and store
for when rain was no more.
The forgotten one saved a nation.
Egypt's bounty caught wind
and Israel would send the brothers to buy grain.
And there Joseph stood, but beyond recognition.
And the memories took reel,
and all he could feel
was joy stained with tremendous pain.
Twice they came trembling
until 11 bowed down,
and Joseph, weeping aloud,
knew what God had done.
They would be saved by the forgotten one
— Israel and the ones who bore guilt —
all the same.
"I am your brother."
A mix of joy stained with fear.
But tears and grace would flow like rain
on the shoulders of shame,
because the one who had died when they lied
was loving them.
What they meant for evil, God meant for good.
His will still stood.
Moving a family tree.

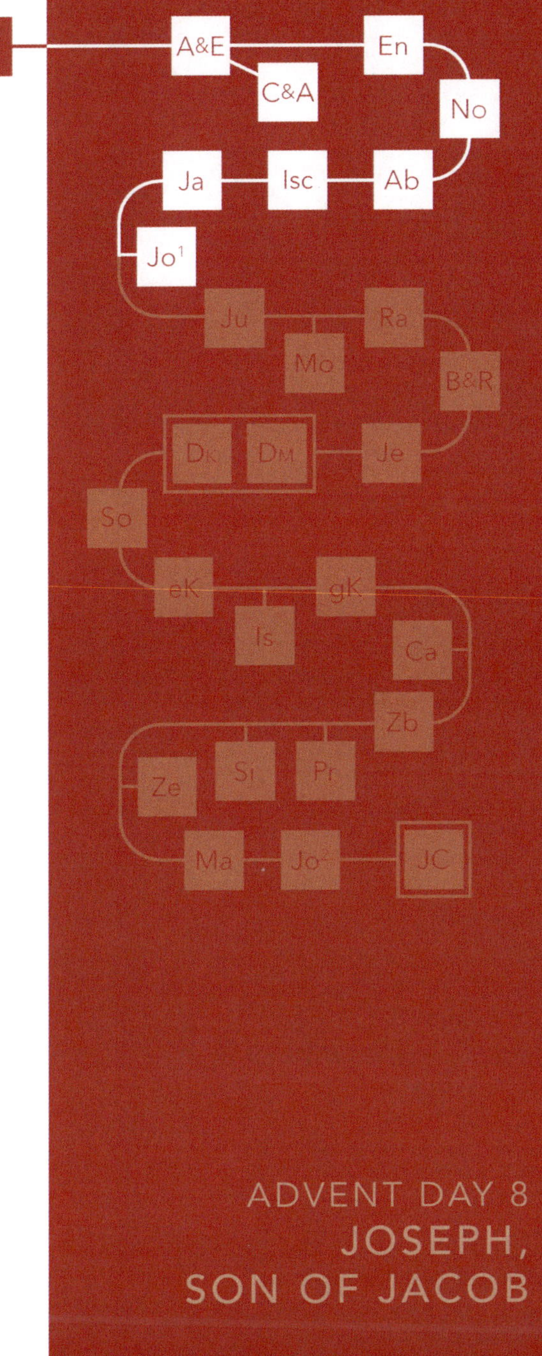

ADVENT DAY 8
JOSEPH, SON OF JACOB

9

JUDAH

The scepter

shall not depart

from Judah.

FROM SCRIPTURE, GOD TELLS HIS STORY...

GENESIS 38:6-7

And Judah took a wife for Er his firstborn, and her name was Tamar. But Er, Judah's firstborn, was wicked in the sight of the Lord, and the Lord put him to death.

Another wicked son (Genesis 38:8-10)

GENESIS 38:11,13-15

Then Judah said to Tamar his daughter-in-law, "Remain a widow in your father's house, till Shelah my son grows up."

...When Tamar was told, "Your father-in-law is going up to Timnah to shear his sheep," she took off her widow's garments and covered herself with a veil, wrapping herself up, and sat at the entrance to Enaim, which is on the road to Timnah. For she saw that Shelah was grown up, and she had not been given to him in marriage. When Judah saw her, he thought she was a prostitute, for she had covered her face.

Judah and Tamar's exchange (Genesis 38:16-25)

GENESIS 38:25-26

And [Tamar] said, "Please identify whose these are, the signet and the cord and the staff." Then Judah identified them and said, "She is more righteous than I, since I did not give her to my son Shelah."

The birth of twins (Genesis 38:27-30)

1 CHRONICLES 2:3-4

The sons of Judah: Er, Onan and Shelah; these three Bath-shua the Canaanite bore to him. Now Er, Judah's firstborn, was evil in the sight of the Lord, and he put him to death. His daughter-in-law Tamar also bore him Perez and Zerah. Judah had five sons in all.

REVELATION 5:5

"Weep no more; behold, the Lion of the tribe of Judah, the Root of David, has conquered."

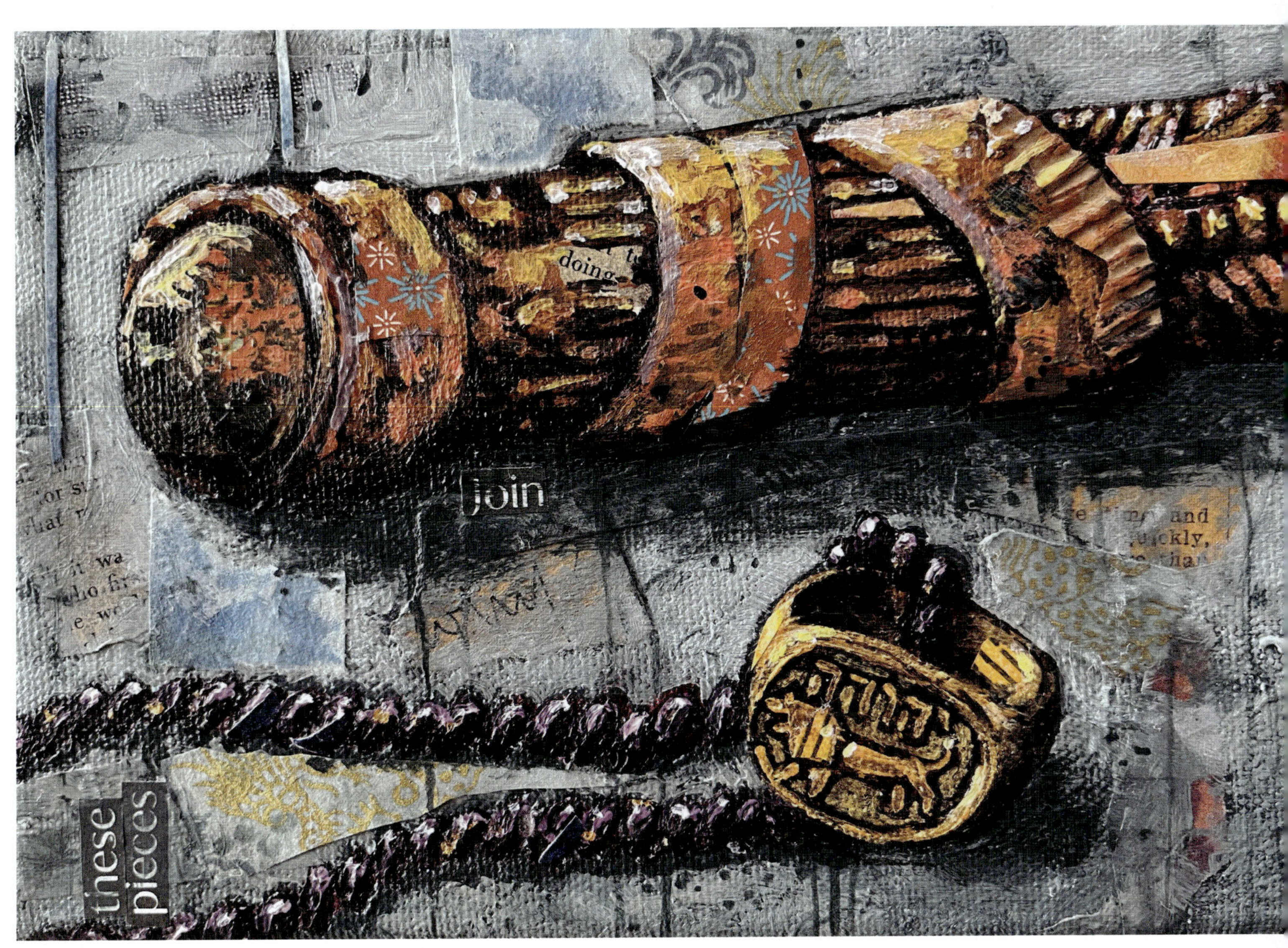
join
these pieces

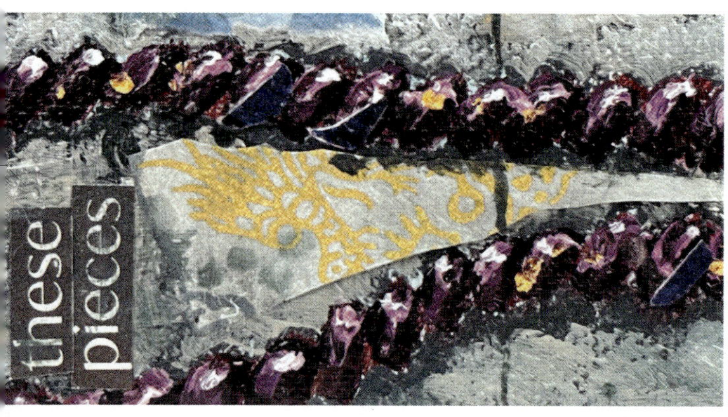

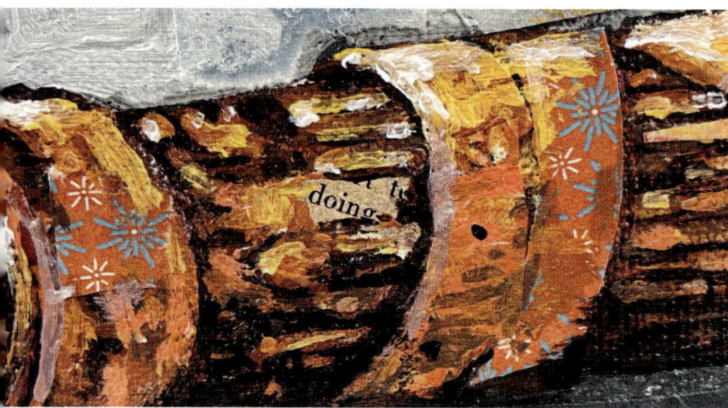

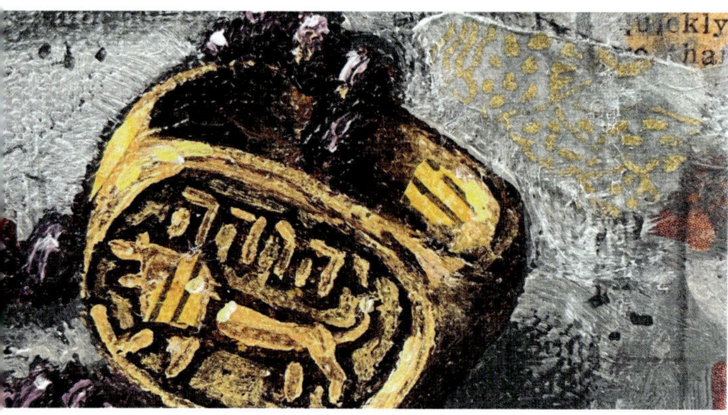

Messianic line through time:
Abraham to Isaac to Jacob to his son.
But Joseph was not the one.
Instead, his older brother Judah
— a surprise.
Prodigal, ready to break free of family ties,
he went down, out of town,
to see the ways of the world.
Married a girl and had three sons.
A home built on sand, in a pagan land.
Er, his oldest, made Tamar his wife.
But his deeds were evil so God took his life,
leaving a widow now — no child.
Judah, wanting an heir,
placed Tamar into his middle son's care.
But what Onen did brought shame,
despised the name he was called to extend.
God too brought his end.
Widow twice and now unprotected.
Judah suspected
death would come to his youngest son
if he married her too.
What was he to do?
Sent her home with a promise to come
after Shelah grew.
"He'll marry you."
No intention to follow through.
She knew.

Time flew.
No call to take her hand.
But news came — Judah's wife had died
and he was coming her way.
A plan.
She removed the black she wore,
wrapped herself in color to the floor.
A veil covered her face;
took a seat of disgrace at the gate and waited.
Judah called.
Didn't recognize the one he'd forgotten.
"What would you give to be comforted?" she asked.
A signet ring and cord,
and in his hand, a staff.
A careless exchange to numb the past.
Then left, like it never happened.
Back in black, Tamar held a secret,
carried new life too — two.
Judah heard and brought her back to be condemned.
Three pieces in the hands of his twice-removed daughter.
"These, I believe, belong to the father."
Shame covered Judah, humility smothered,
but grace reigned in this line.
Twins came in time.
Through one son a breach would break into the dark,
bind up the broken heart.
A coming king in Zion,
from this tribe of Judah — a lion.

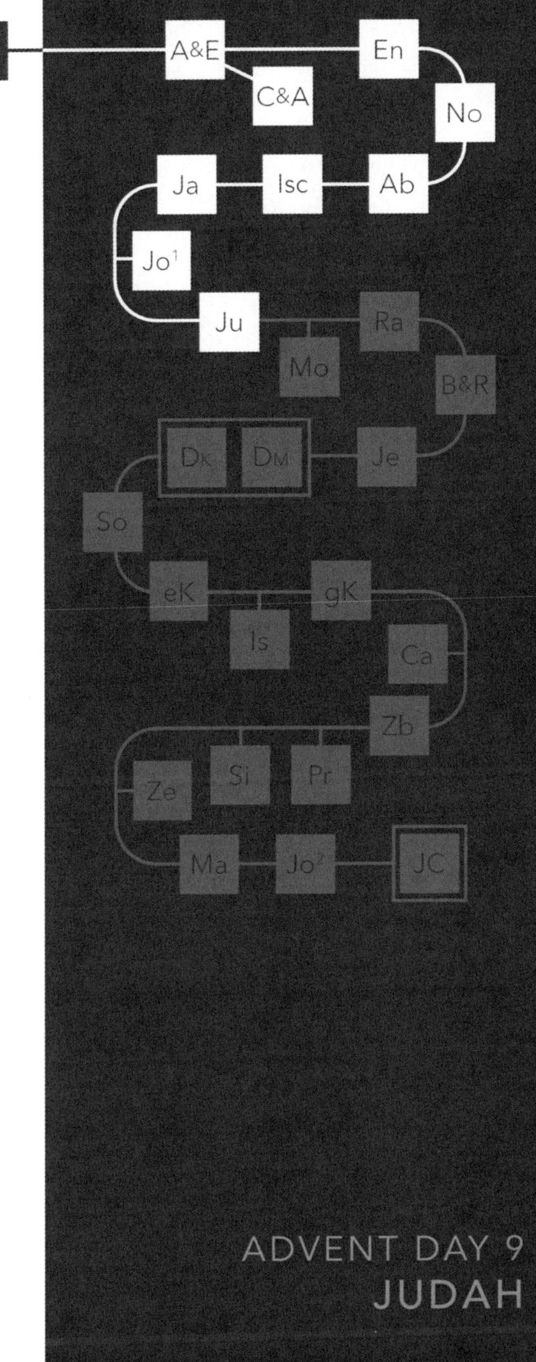

ADVENT DAY 9
JUDAH

10

MOSES

The LORD used to speak to Moses face to face, as a man speaks to his friend.

FROM SCRIPTURE, GOD TELLS HIS STORY...

New pharaoh, new plan (Exodus 1)
Moses is hidden (Exodus 2:1-10)

EXODUS 2:5-10

Now the daughter of Pharaoh came down to bathe at the river, while her young women walked beside the river. She saw the basket among the reeds and sent her servant woman, and she took it.When she opened it, she saw the child, and behold, the baby was crying. She took pity on him and said, "This is one of the Hebrews' children." Then his sister said to Pharaoh's daughter, "Shall I go and call you a nurse from the Hebrew women to nurse the child for you?" And Pharaoh's daughter said to her, "Go." So the girl went and called the child's mother. And Pharaoh's daughter said to her, "Take this child away and nurse him for me, and I will give you your wages." So the woman took the child and nursed him. When the child grew older, she brought him to Pharaoh's daughter, and he became her son. She named him Moses, "Because," she said, "I drew him out of the water."

Moses flees (Exodus 2:11-25)
Called to return (Exodus 3:1-4:17)

EXODUS 3:3-10

Moses said, "I will turn aside to see this great sight, why the bush is not burned." ... God called to him out of the bush, "Moses, Moses!" And he said, "Here I am." Then he said, "Do not come near; take your sandals off your feet, for the place on which you are standing is holy ground." And he said, "I am the God of your father, the God of Abraham, the God of Isaac, and the God of Jacob." And Moses hid his face, for he was afraid to look at God.

Then the Lord said, "I have surely seen the affliction of my people who are in Egypt and have heard their cry ... Come, I will send you to Pharaoh that you may bring my people, the children of Israel, out of Egypt."

Rejection (Exodus 5:1-7:13)
Plagues and Passover (Exodus 7:14-12:51)
Through the sea (Exodus 14:1-15:21)
To the mountain (Exodus 15:22-19:25)
Clear commands (Exodus 20; 24:1-13)
Near the land (Numbers 13-14)
In the desert (Numbers 20:1-26:1-4,63-65; Deuteronomy 1:1-4:40)
Last words (Deuteronomy 29:2-34:8)

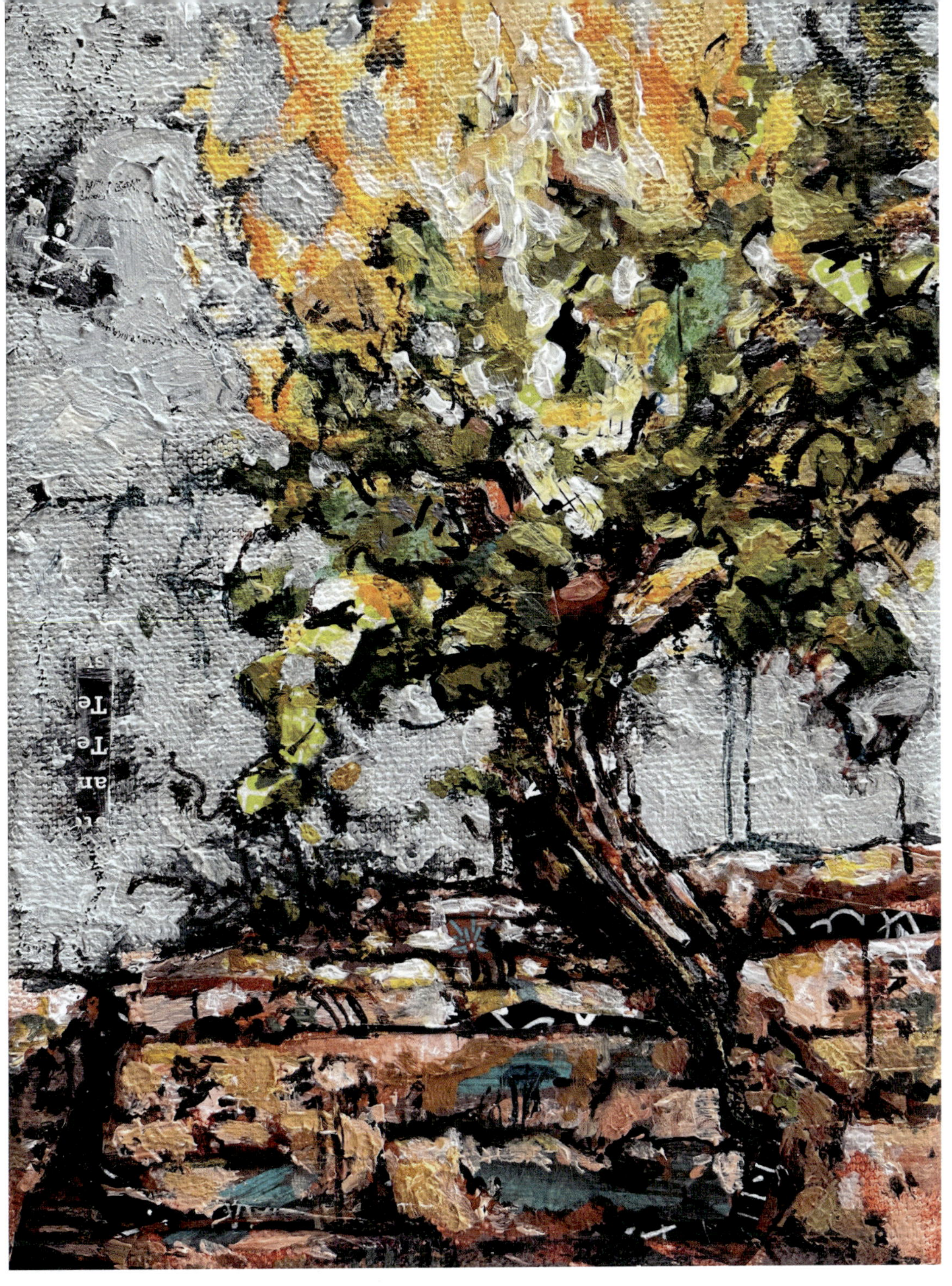

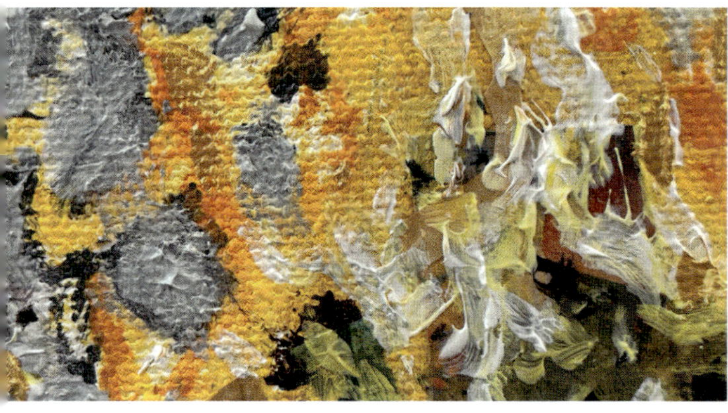

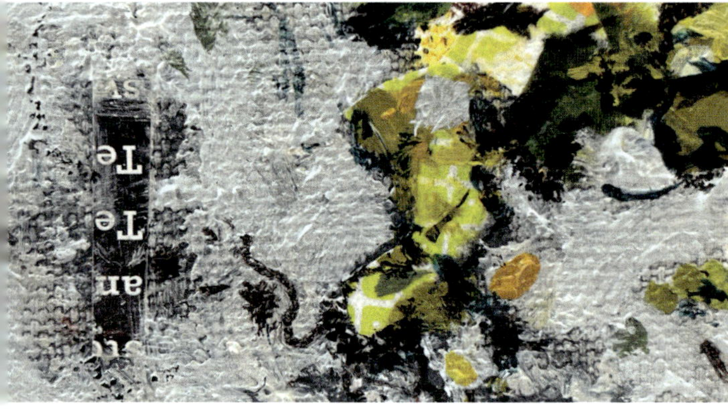

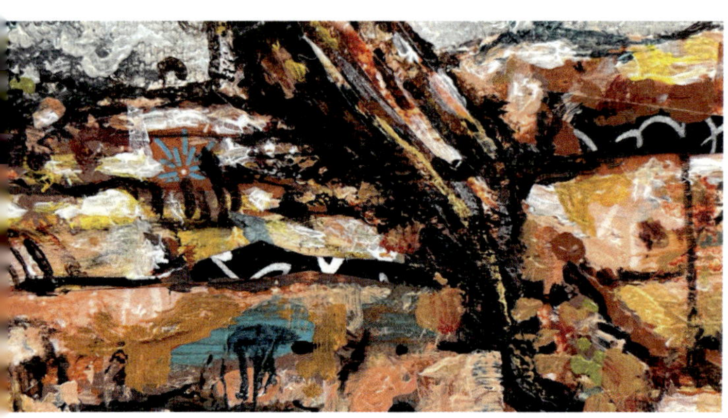

Centuries in a foreign land,
Israel's tree would expand
exponentially.
Pharaoh's fear too.
He would sow a plan with a heavy hand,
to reap Egypt's favor.
Overwhelming labor,
oppression,
for the sake of a pure nation.
Cries of the broken, who seemed forgotten,
would be heard by their Father.
The edicts got harder.
Boys would die.
But among reeds high, a baby's cry.
Hidden, then found.
Moses drawn out.
Now a son of the Crown.
Forty years, but truth came around and he fled.
Pharaoh raged.
Time aged.
Moses gauged his next step.
Bush aflame, but unsinged.
God spoke His name.
Moses unhinged.
"Go get My people from that land."
Shaky hand and tongue, he approached the one who said
"No!" nine times
after plagues and signs.

Finally, death would come to the firstborn sons
of all who were not covered
when Judgment passed over Egypt's land,
releasing Pharaoh's hand.
Magnifying I Am.
Israel delivered.

Moses led them
through the Sea to the Mountain
where a Law was written in stone.
But hearts would roam
and Moses would plead their case,
grace after grace.
He led them out from that place
to the land promised,
not through.
They doubted God was right,
refused to fight.
Wandered the desert instead.
Wondering.
Tabernacles, tents, the manna God sent.
For 40 years
until children learned from parents' mistakes.
Moses would lead them all the way
to where he could see the place he could not stay.
But since the day his heart burned at the flame,
when I Am called his name,
it had *all* been holy ground.

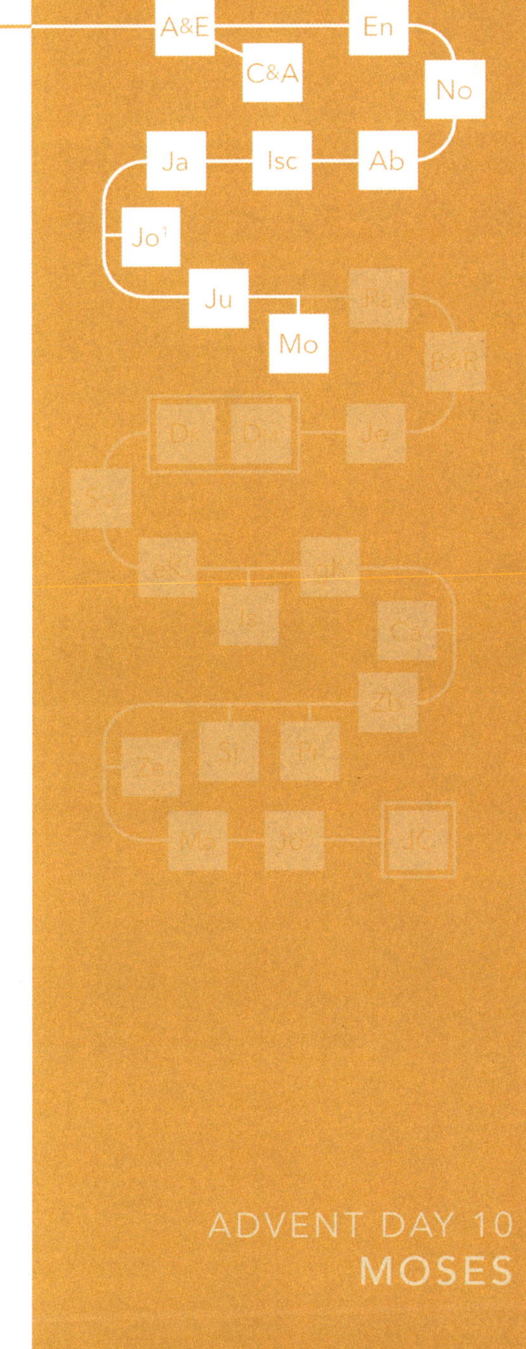

ADVENT DAY 10
MOSES

11

RAHAB

He is God

in the heavens

above and on

the earth beneath.

FROM SCRIPTURE, GOD TELLS HIS STORY...

JOSHUA 2:1, 8-9, 11-15, 18

And Joshua the son of Nun sent two men secretly from Shittim as spies, saying, "Go, view the land, especially Jericho." And they went and came into the house of a prostitute whose name was Rahab and lodged there.

...Before the men lay down, she came up to them on the roof and said to the men, "I know that the Lord has given you the land, and that the fear of you has fallen upon us, and that all the inhabitants of the land melt away before you ... For the Lord your God, he is God in the heavens above and on the earth beneath. Now then, please swear to me by the Lord that, as I have dealt kindly with you, you also will deal kindly with my father's house, and give me a sure sign that you will save alive my father and mother, my brothers and sisters, and all who belong to them, and deliver our lives from death." And the men said to her, "Our life for yours even to death! If you do not tell this business of ours, then when the Lord gives us the land we will deal kindly and faithfully with you."

Then she let them down by a rope through the window, for her house was built into the city wall, so that she lived in the wall ...The men said to her, "Behold, when we come into the land, you shall tie this scarlet cord in the window through which you let us down."

The day the walls came down (Joshua 6:1-21)

JOSHUA 6:22-25

But to the two men who had spied out the land, Joshua said, "Go into the prostitute's house and bring out from there the woman and all who belong to her, as you swore to her." So the young men who had been spies went in and brought out Rahab and her father and mother and brothers and all who belonged to her. And they brought all her relatives and put them outside the camp of Israel. And they burned the city with fire, and everything in it.

...But Rahab the prostitute and her father's household and all who belonged to her, Joshua saved alive. And she has lived in Israel to this day, because she hid the messengers whom Joshua sent to spy out Jericho.

JAMES 2:25

And in the same way was not also Rahab the prostitute justified by works when she received the messengers and sent them out by another way?

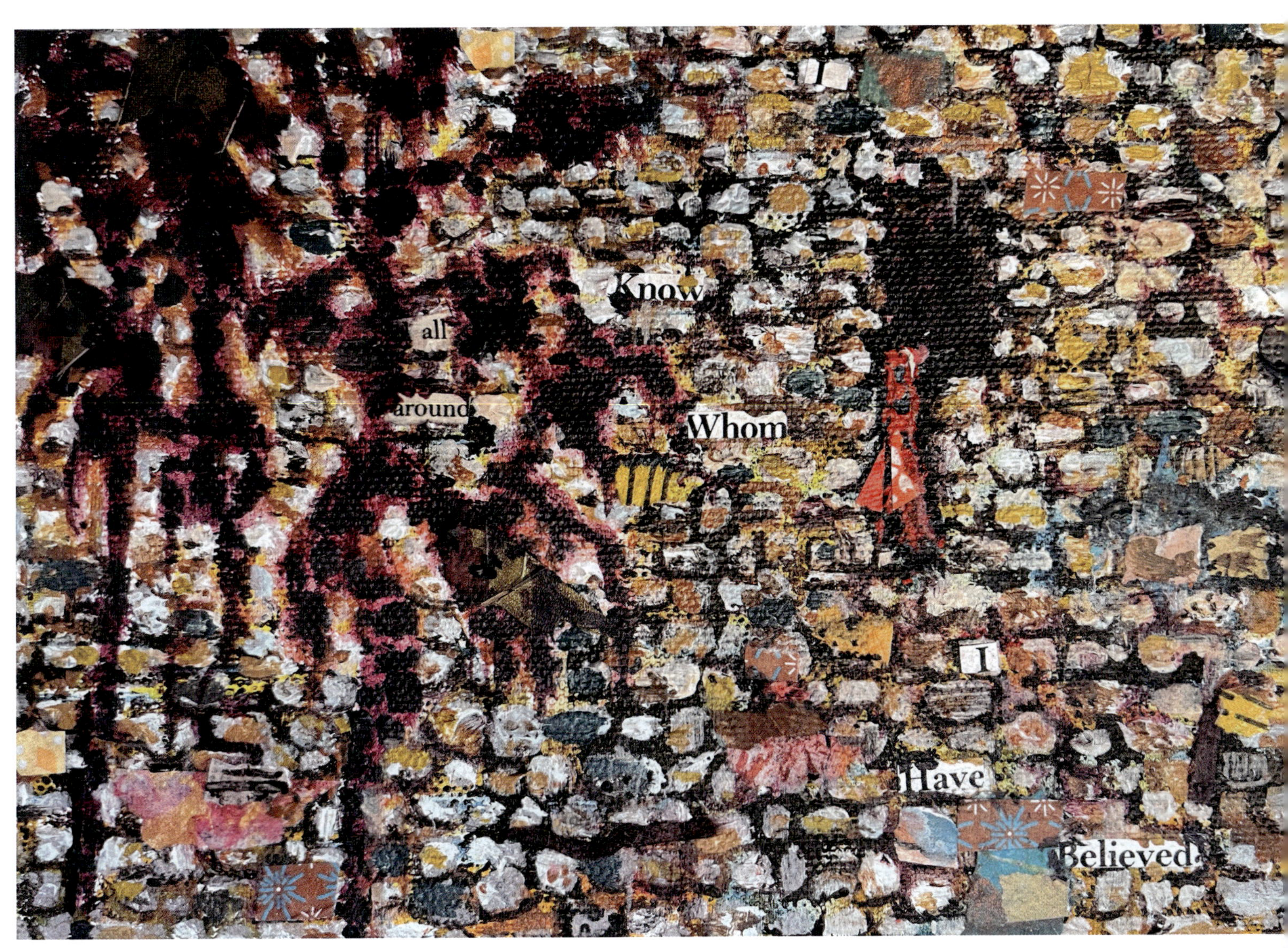
Know
all
around
Whom
I
Have
Believed

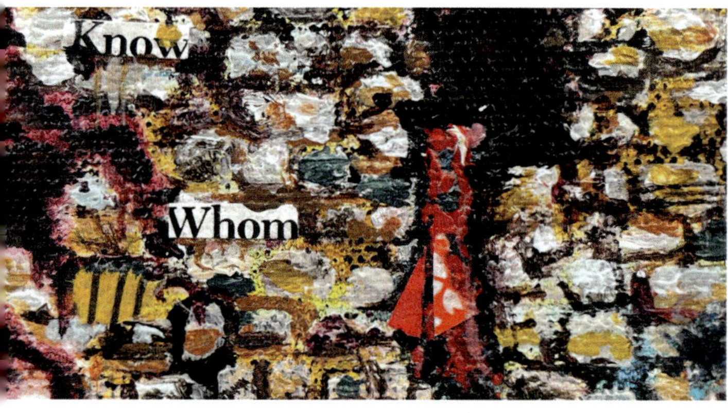

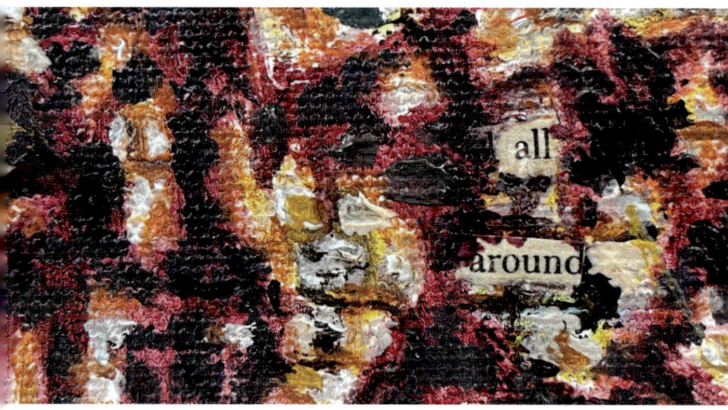

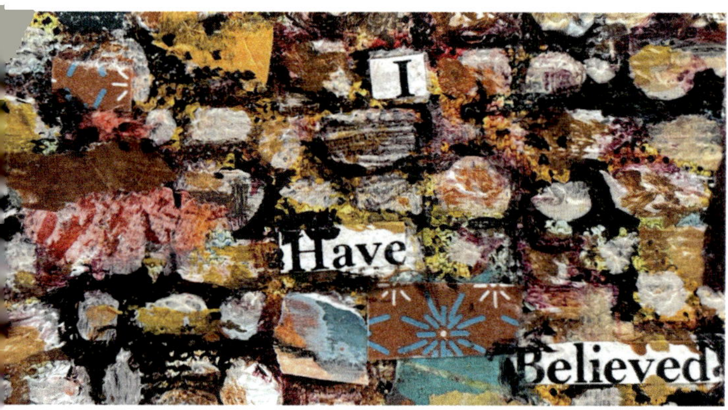

All of Israel stood at the border
of the promised land,
inhabited by men who caused such fear
in the generation before.
Joshua followed in Moses's steps
to lead and heed
everything God said.
Now on the Jordan riverbed,
with Jericho's walls looming ahead,
they deliberated battle plans.
Spies sent in.
Took cover within a home on the wall.
Rahab — a woman of the Fall
who lived on the fringes of society and town.
Now, tinges of hope.
She didn't doubt the timing;
God had been priming her fear
to believe.
Among people blind,
only she could see the I Am.
He was the God
of *them*.
She hid the spies from searching eyes,
then confessed she knew
what God would do to her city.
They were all dead men,
the whole land.
Against God, who could stand?

"The Lord, your God,
rules the heavens above and the earth beneath.
Could He...
would He also save me?"
A promise made
that on the day Israel arrived
a red cord should be tied
from the window outside,
marking *her.*
When the wall was breached,
her house they would reach
to rescue her from the fall.
And on that day
when the walls gave way,
a harlot moved from dark to light.
The one who was bought over and over
was sought by One who loved her
and showed her.
"Them" became "we,"
part of a family tree,
set apart at the start of it all.
Took Salmon's hand, one from Judah's clan,
one branch closer to the chosen Seed.
An outside woman,
a scarlet thread,
was stitched from the beginning of time
into Messiah's line.

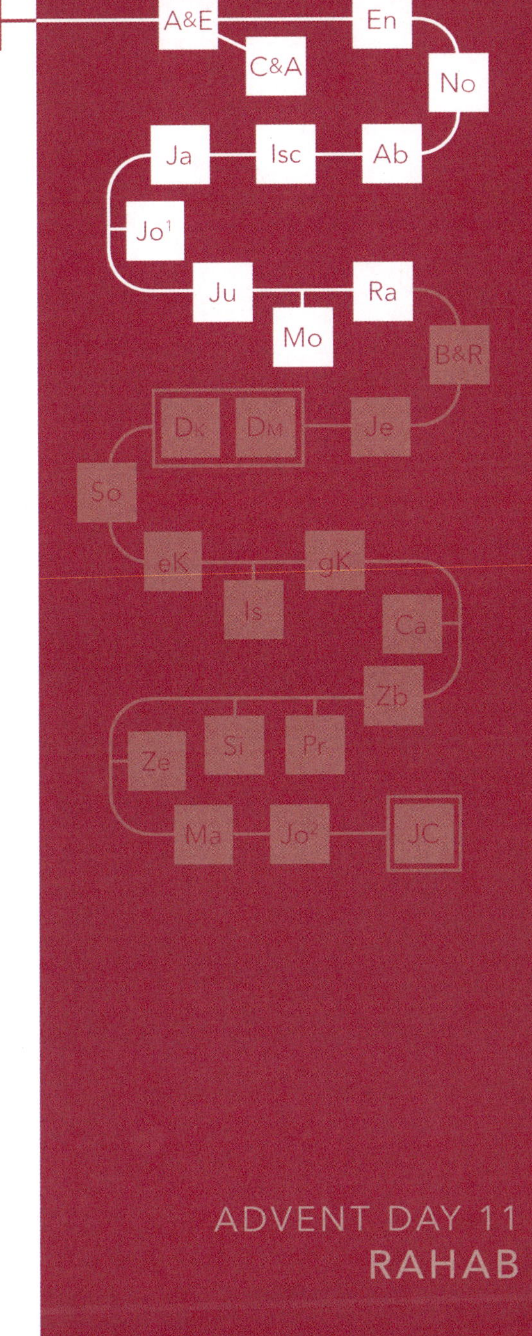

12

BOAZ AND RUTH

Your people

shall be my people,

and your God

my God.

FROM SCRIPTURE, GOD TELLS HIS STORY...

Three widows (Ruth 1:1-5)
Return home (Ruth 1:8-22)

RUTH 1:16-18

Ruth said, "Do not urge me to leave you or to return from following you. For where you go I will go, and where you lodge I will lodge. Your people shall be my people, and your God my God. Where you die I will die, and there will I be buried. May the Lord do so to me and more also if anything but death parts me from you."

RUTH 1:20-21

"Do not call me Naomi; call me Mara, for the Almighty has dealt very bitterly with me. I went away full, and the Lord has brought me back empty.

Ruth in Boaz's field (Ruth 2)

RUTH 2:11-12

Then [Ruth] fell on her face, bowing to the ground, and said to him, "Why have I found favor in your eyes, that you should take notice of me, since I am a foreigner?" But Boaz answered her, "All that you have done for your mother-in-law since the death of your husband has been fully told to me, and how you left your father and mother and your native land and came to a people that you did not know before. The LORD repay you for what you have done, and a full reward be given you by the LORD, the God of Israel, under whose wings you have come to take refuge!"

Ruth at Boaz's feet (Ruth 3)
Boaz redeems (Ruth 4:1-12)

RUTH 4:13-15, 16

So Boaz took Ruth, and she became his wife ... Then the women said to Naomi, "Blessed be the LORD, who has not left you this day without a redeemer, and may his name be renowned in Israel! He shall be to you a restorer of life and a nourisher of your old age, for your daughter-in-law who loves you, who is more to you than seven sons, has given birth to him."

... They named him Obed. He was the father of Jesse, the father of David.

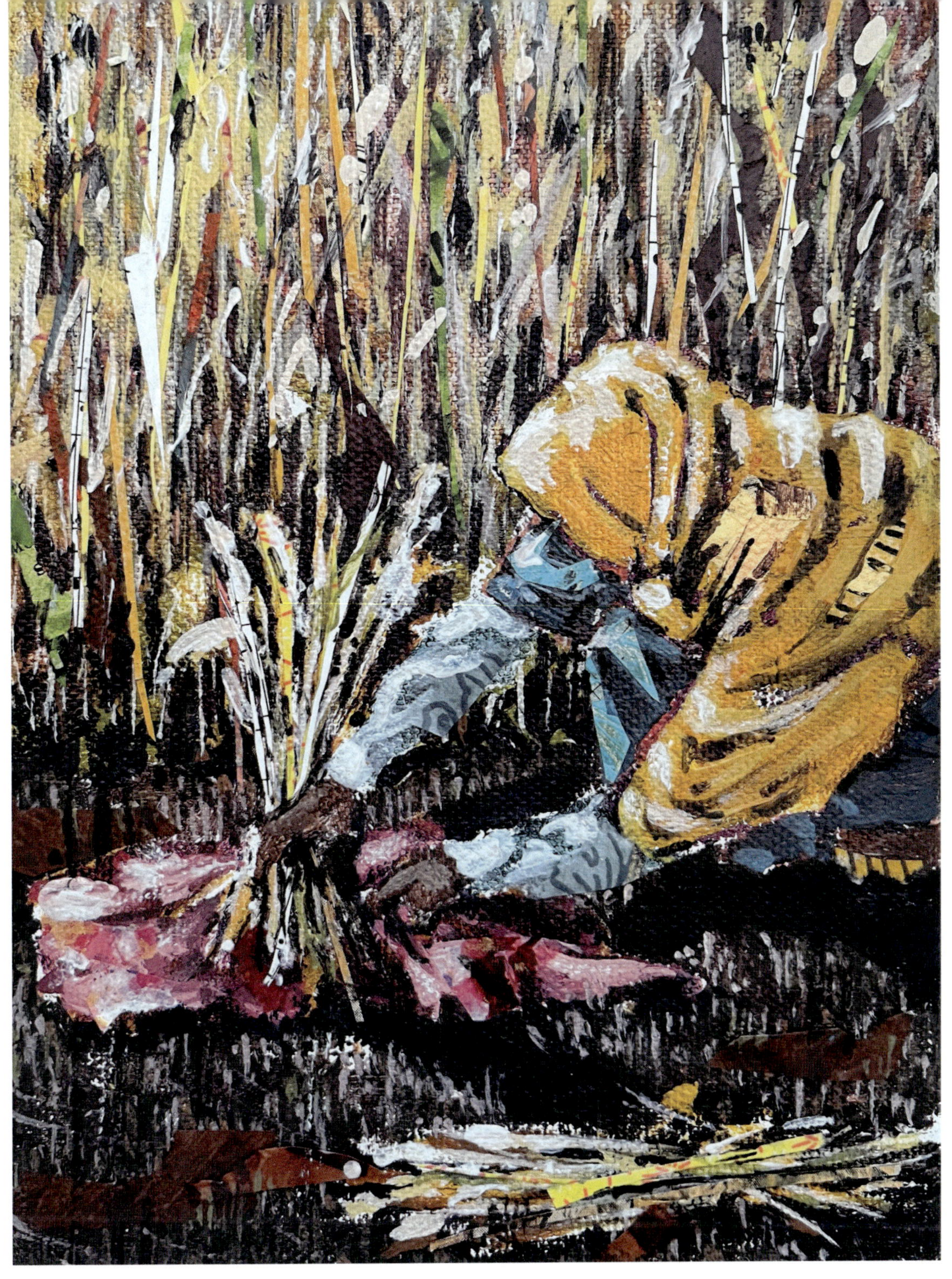

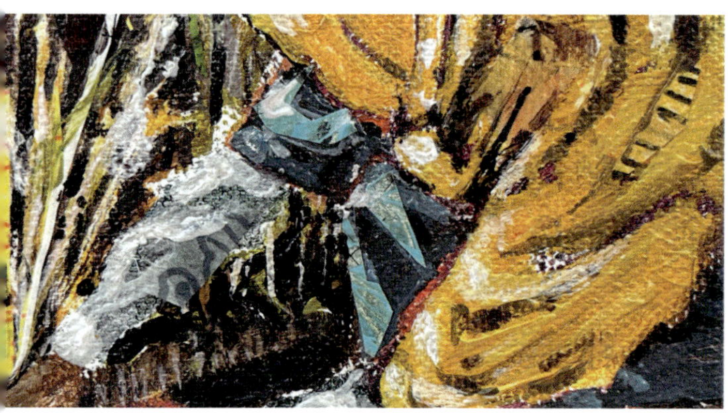

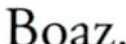

Boaz.
Son of Rahab, older now.
Husband and father to none,
but he had won the favor
of all who worked his land.
A righteous man.
High reputation ushered praise.
Boaz — a man set in his ways.

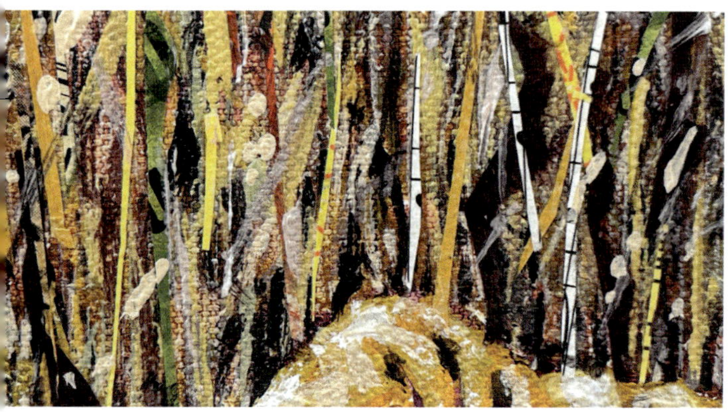

Naomi.
Mother-in-law, mourning now.
Widow and mother to two sons, now gone.
She despised her name and wore her shame
like a black veil.
A woman unwell.
Calamity had hit her.
Naomi — a woman who was bitter.

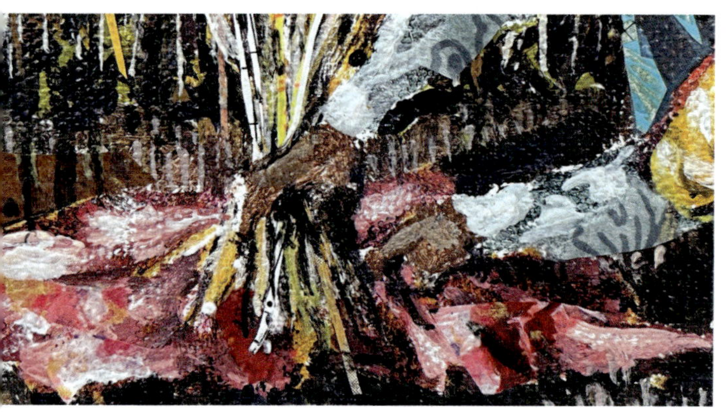

Ruth.
Daughter-in-law, widow now.
To Naomi she would cling
and face whatever life would bring.
Trust her God and His provision.
Ruth — a foreigner in poor position.

Ruth found she could work the field
and gather the yield left behind,
to glean unseen.

But the owner *did* see.
"Who is she?" Boaz inquired
from the men he hired.
And her story they would tell.
"Naomi" rang a bell
and favor fell on Ruth that day.
She would relay to Naomi
the bounty received from the man
she perceived as gracious and kind.
That name came to mind.
Naomi's kin.
Was God bringing him in?
And Hope took a seat at the table.
At night, again out of sight,
Ruth laid at the feet of a man
who believed he was past
his season of blessing.
Boaz recognized grace that day and made a way
to redeem his bride and his kin.
And again, God shook these three
off the paths they were taking.
Ruth, He would cover,
and Boaz would love her,
and Naomi learned once more how to sing.
A child God would bring,
— the grandfather of a ruddy king.

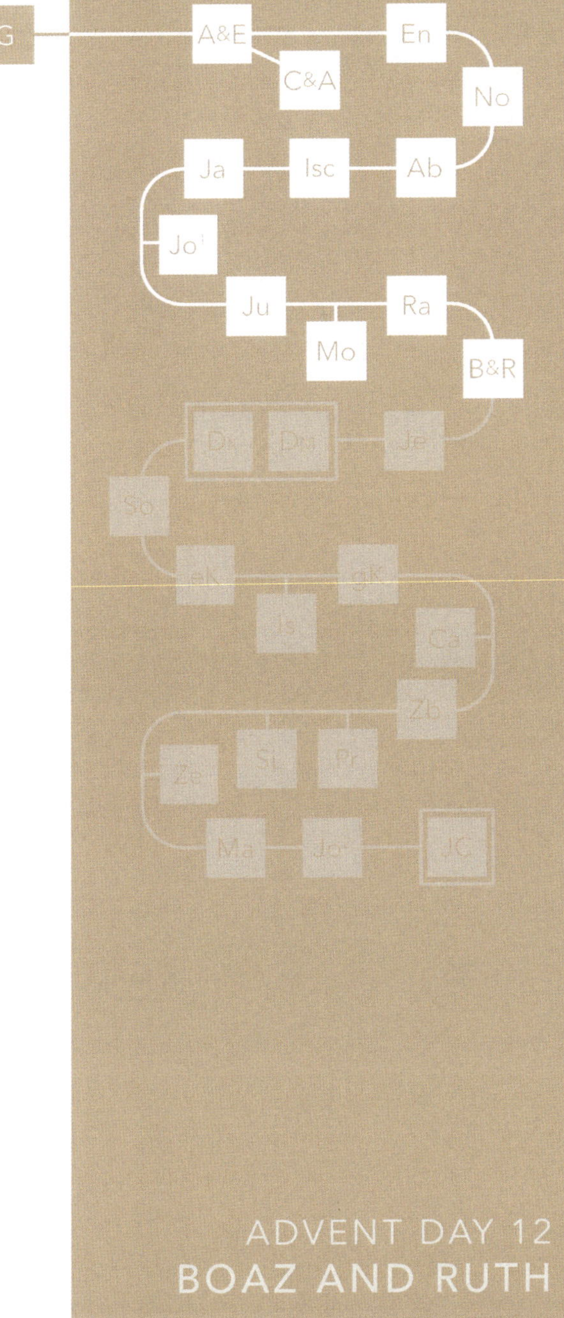

13

JESSE

...a shoot from the stump of Jesse, and a branch from his roots shall bear fruit.

FROM SCRIPTURE, GOD TELLS HIS STORY...

1 SAMUEL 16:5-13

[Samuel] consecrated Jesse and his sons and invited them to the sacrifice. When they came, he looked on Eliab and thought, "Surely the Lord's anointed is before him." But the Lord said to Samuel, "Do not look on his appearance or on the height of his stature, because I have rejected him. For the Lord sees not as man sees: man looks on the outward appearance, but the Lord looks on the heart." Then Jesse called Abinadab and made him pass before Samuel. And he said, "Neither has the Lord chosen this one." Then Jesse made Shammah pass by. And he said, "Neither has the Lord chosen this one." And Jesse made seven of his sons pass before Samuel. And Samuel said to Jesse, "The Lord has not chosen these." Then Samuel said to Jesse, "Are all your sons here?" And he said, "There remains yet the youngest, but behold, he is keeping the sheep." And Samuel said to Jesse, "Send and get him, for we will not sit down till he comes here." And he sent and brought him in. Now he was ruddy and had beautiful eyes and was handsome. And the Lord said, "Arise, anoint him, for this is he." Then Samuel took the horn of oil and anointed him in the midst of his brothers. And the Spirit of the Lord rushed upon David from that day forward.

ACTS 13:21-22

Then they asked for a king, and God gave them Saul ... for forty years. And when [God] had removed him, he raised up David to be their king, of whom he testified and said, "I have found in David the son of Jesse a man after my heart, who will do all my will."

HEBREWS 11:1

There shall come forth a shoot from the stump of Jesse, and a branch from his roots shall bear fruit.

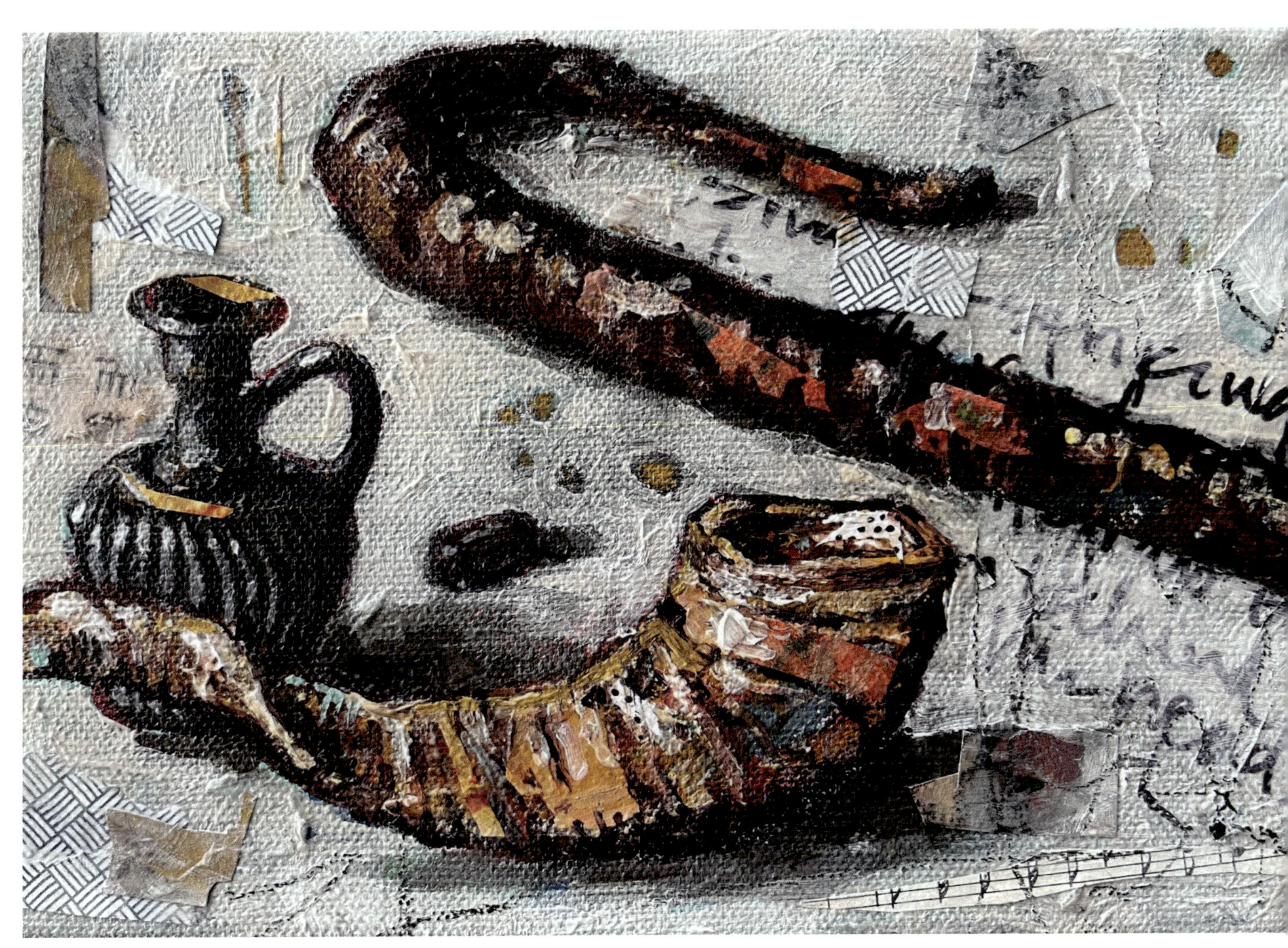

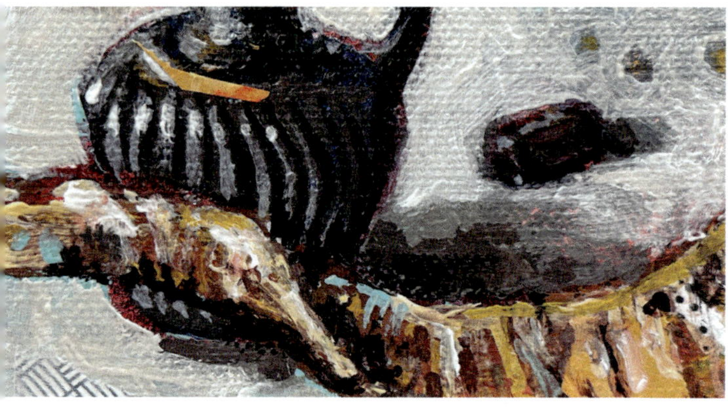

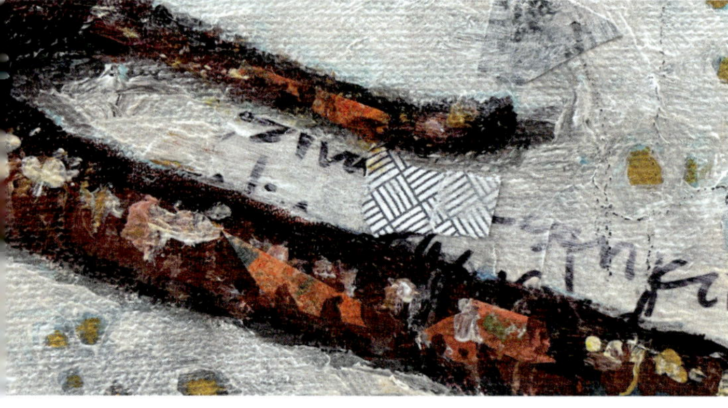

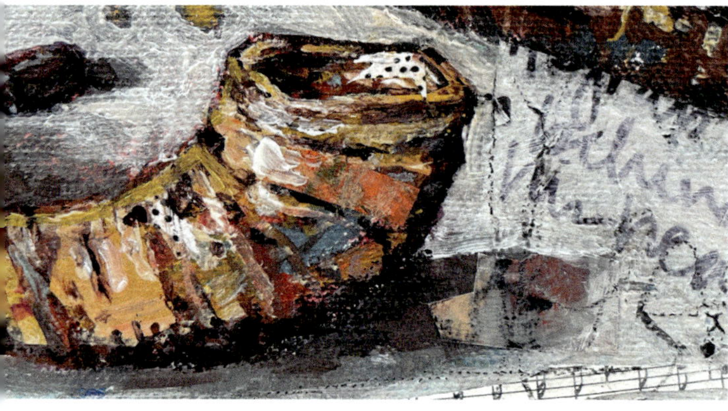

They wanted a king,
one with power to lead,
bring their nation up to speed
with everyone else.
Samuel, the prophet and judge,
disagreed.
God could see the end,
even when they rejected Him,
but told Samuel to proceed with their request.
Man thought it best that Saul would rule.
Tall and smart.
On the outside, he fit the part.
But after taking the throne,
he was overcome with fear
and would forge his own way down.
God would reject the Crown.
So the prophet was given another task.
"Go anoint another,
but *I* will pick the man.
Find Jesse's family in Bethlehem."
The grandson of Boaz and Ruth
had eight sons and one
would suit as king.
One-by-one, Jesse presented his boys,
winsom and fit.
But that was not it.
God said, "No," again and again.
He chose none of them.

The prophet pressed in,
"Have you no more sons?"
Jesse had forgotten one,
"My youngest,
still in the field with the sheep."
When the boy was brought in,
Samuel stood.
"That's him."
What God sees
is more than skin deep.
Samuel took the ram's horn of oil
and anointed the boy's head.
His scepter
— a crook and rod instead.
God's spirit would leave the current king
and be given to a boy
who could play and sing.
A branch from Jesse's tree would spring up
and a shepherd would lead them.

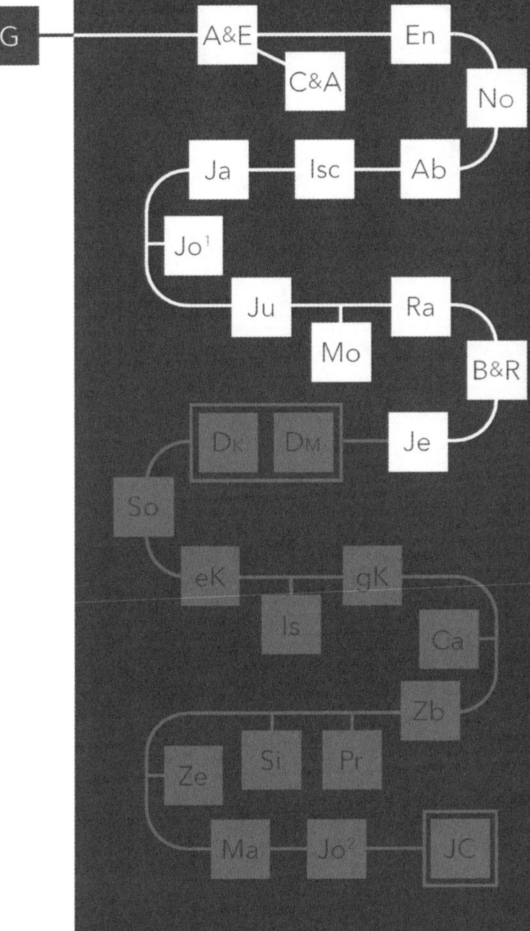

ADVENT DAY 13
JESSE

14

DAVID, THE MUSICIAN

My heart is steadfast, O God! I will sing and make melody with all my being!

FROM SCRIPTURE, GOD TELLS HIS STORY...

1 SAMUEL 16:17-22

[King] Saul said to his servants, "Provide for me a man who can play well and bring him to me." One of the young men answered, "Behold, I have seen a son of Jesse the Bethlehemite, who is skillful in playing, a man of valor, a man of war, prudent in speech, and a man of good presence, and the Lord is with him." Therefore Saul sent messengers to Jesse and said, "Send me David your son, who is with the sheep." And Jesse took a donkey laden with bread and a skin of wine and a young goat and sent them by David his son to Saul. And David came to Saul and entered his service. And Saul loved him greatly, and he became his armor-bearer. And Saul sent to Jesse, saying, "Let David remain in my service, for he has found favor in my sight."

"How Majestic" (Psalm 8)
"How Long?" (Psalm 13)
"Have Mercy" (Psalm 51)
"Save Me" (Psalm 69)

2 SAMUEL 22:1

And David spoke to the Lord the words of this song on the day when the Lord delivered him from the hand of all his enemies, and from the hand of Saul.

"Bless the Lord" (Psalm 103)
"I Was Glad" (Psalm 122)
"O Lord, You Know" (Psalm 139)
"Praise Him" (Psalm 150)

2 SAMUEL 23:1

Now these are the last words of David:

The oracle of David, the son of Jesse, the oracle of the man who was raised on high, the anointed of the God of Jacob, the sweet psalmist of Israel.

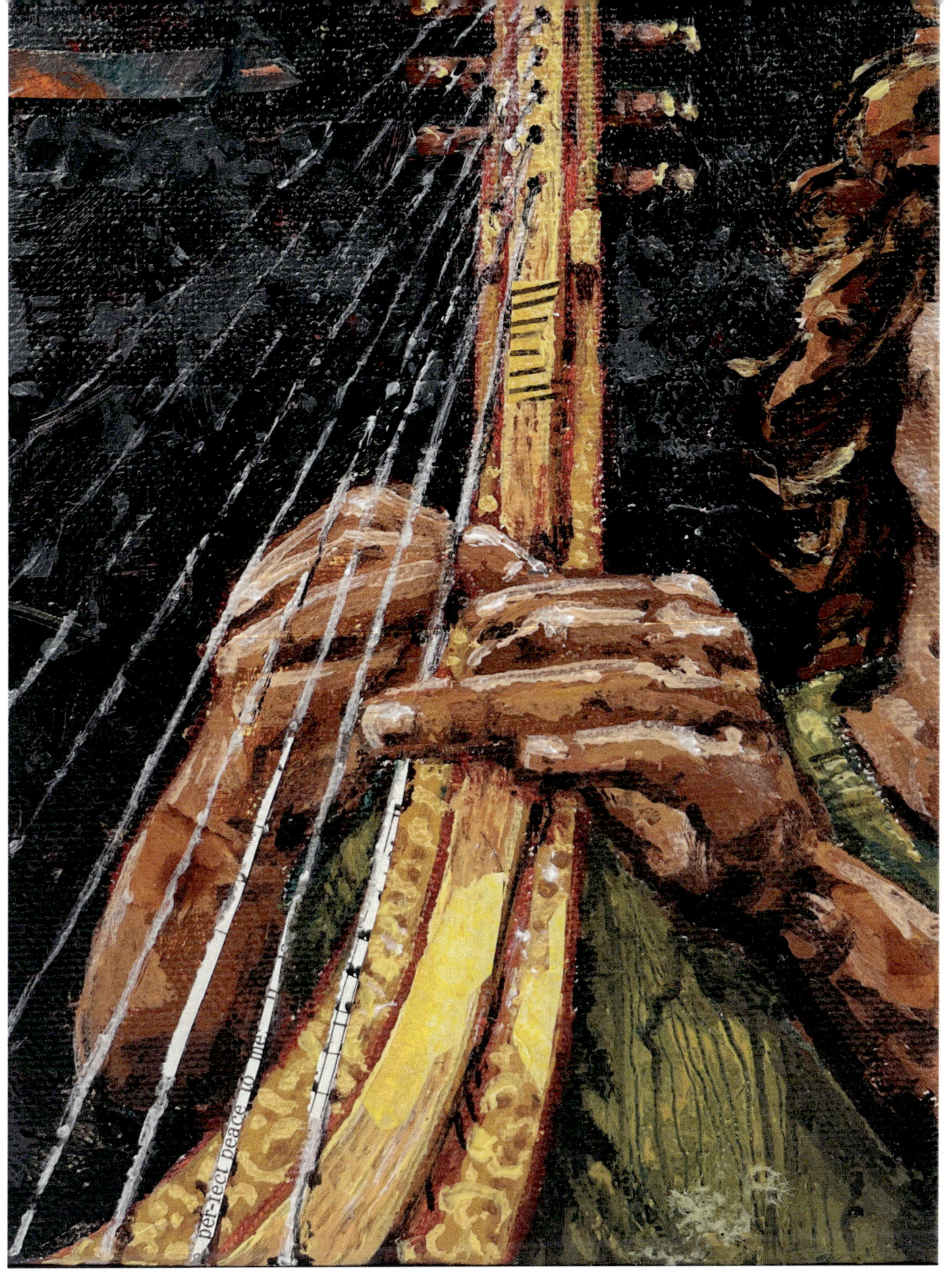
per-fect peace to me

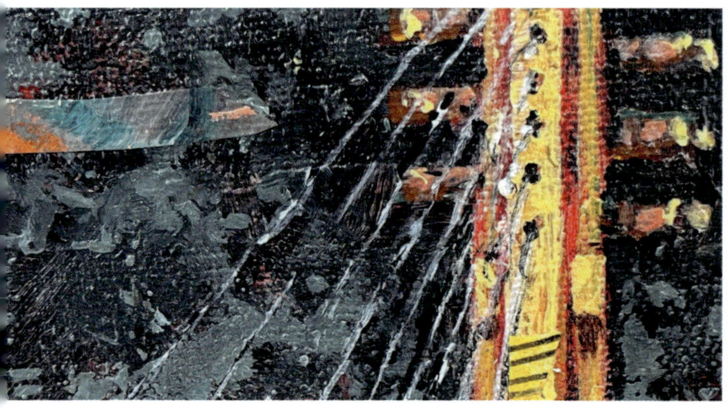

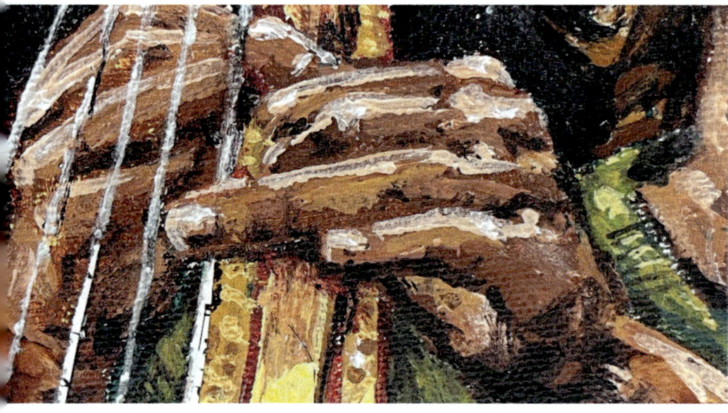

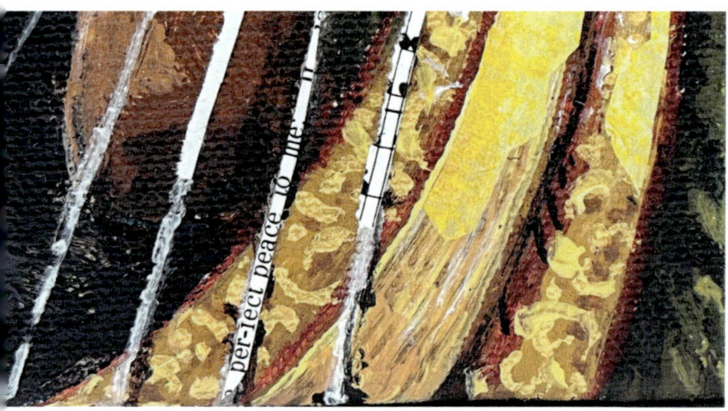

The same hands that slayed
a lion and bear
could strum the strings of a harp and care
for an unstable king.
The same hands that picked up
a sling and five stones
could write songs
in minor tones of lament
and major tones of praise.
The same voice that would raise accusation
to the defiant giant of the Philistine nation
could pour melody
into the parched, secret places of the soul.
David, the one who would be king
could sing and form the words
we could not articulate
into beautiful meter that would dictate
our disoriented hearts.
David's hymns
laid the full breadth of him bare.
Exposed
so that God's people could share
in the sighings,
confessions,
thanksgivings,
and depressions of man.

What is man that God
would be mindful of him
and yet still crown him with glory?
David would tell that story.
Even in the dark,
the shepherd-warrior-king
could not hide from the One who was light.
David knew that was right,
so he wrote it.
And when sin and shame
covered every inch of David's crown,
he found he could scribble down
his broken cries
and carry us to the One
who forgives.
Before a word was on his tongue,
his Lord knew it.
How precious that was to him.
And a hymn would begin.
Even in the waiting and hiding,
he'd be writing what is true.
A song composed just for you.
By his emptying,
we would be filled.
David,
"the sweet psalmist of Israel."

ADVENT DAY 14

DAVID, THE MUSICIAN

15

DAVID, THE KING

Your throne shall be established forever.

FROM SCRIPTURE, GOD TELLS HIS STORY...

PSALM 2:1-8

Why do the nations rage and the peoples plot in vain?
The kings of the earth set themselves, and the rulers take counsel together,
against the Lord and against his Anointed, saying,
"Let us burst their bonds apart and cast away their cords from us."
He who sits in the heavens laughs; the Lord holds them in derision.

Then he will speak to them in his wrath,
and terrify them in his fury, saying,
"As for me, I have set my King on Zion, my holy hill."

The Lord said to me, "You are my Son; today I have begotten you.
Ask of me, and I will make the nations your heritage,
and the ends of the earth your possession.
You shall break them with a rod of iron
and dash them in pieces like a potter's vessel."

Now therefore, O kings, be wise; be warned, O rulers of the earth.
Serve the LORD with fear, and rejoice with trembling.
Kiss the Son, lest he be angry, and you perish in the way,
for his wrath is quickly kindled.
Blessed are all who take refuge in him.

PSALM 16:2

I say to the Lord, "You are my Lord; I have no good apart from you."

ACTS 13:17-23

The God of this people Israel chose our fathers and made the people great during their stay in the land of Egypt, and with uplifted arm he led them out of it. And for about forty years he put up with them in the wilderness. And after destroying seven nations in the land of Canaan, he gave them their land as an inheritance. All this took about 450 years. And after that he gave them judges until Samuel the prophet. Then they asked for a king, and God gave them Saul the son of Kish, a man of the tribe of Benjamin, for forty years. And when he had removed him, he raised up David to be their king, of whom he testified and said, "I have found in David the son of Jesse a man after my heart, who will do all my will." Of this man's offspring God has brought to Israel a Savior, Jesus, as he promised.

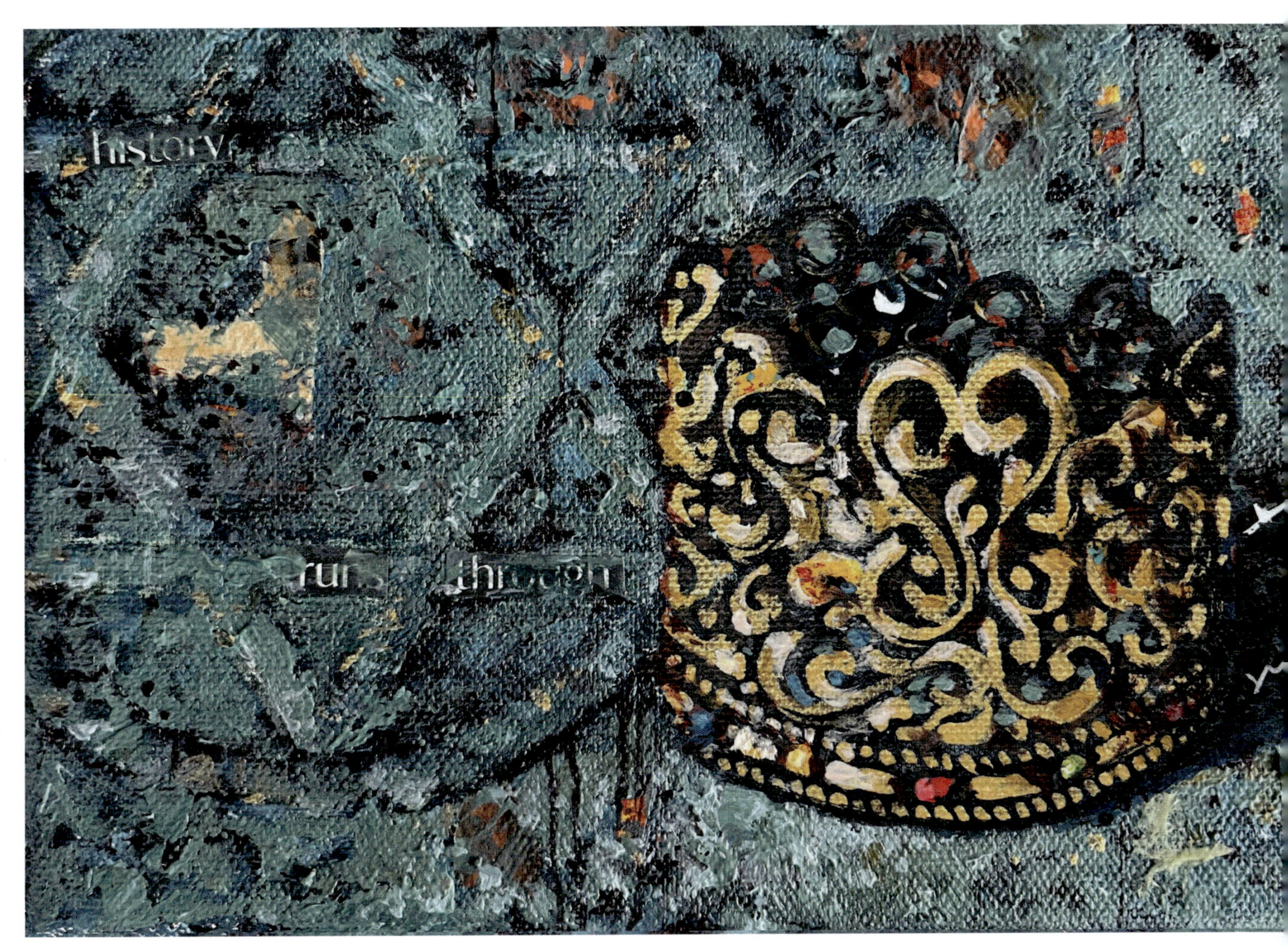
history

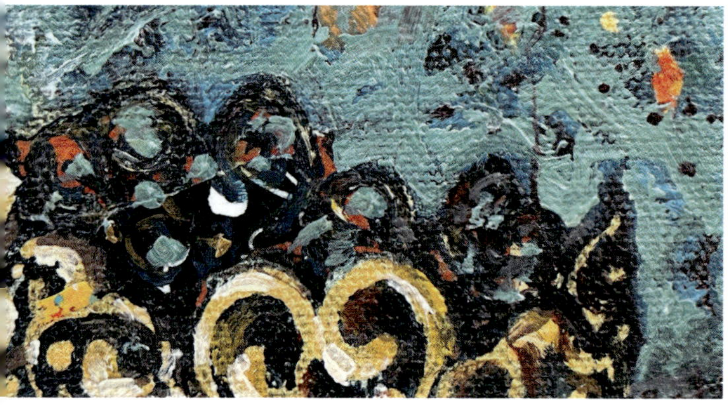

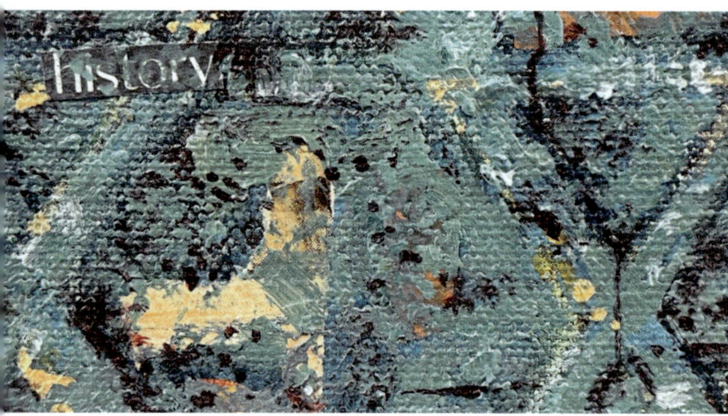

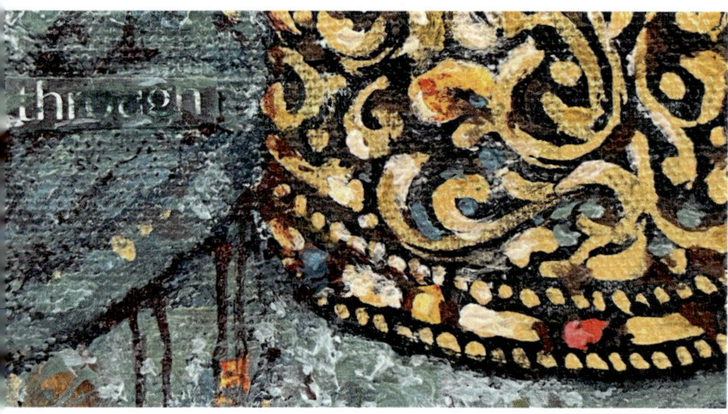

Every day David reigned
was a day God ordained,
written in his story.
After the glory and burden of the throne,
David, now old, had done God's will...
still.
His last words would elevate another King.
One more song he'd sing as he set his crown down.
Jesse's son,
— the one Samuel anointed —
pointed to the Anointed One,
a future Son rising and causing
His kingdom to grow.
That King was Israel's hope.
David understood he had no good
but God alone.
The One who took David's enemy down
with just one stone.
The One who washed away the blood
on David's hands and his bed of sin,
created a clean heart within.
David's Lord was the King on this holy hill...
still.
The One who lifted David's head
when all hope was dead.

The One whose very presence
would cause the king to dance undignified,
or meet the enemy on the other side,
or be still and know.
David's King was still in control.
The One who collected the tears
after years of a family broken.
The One who had spoken a covenant
which David had no right to claim.
His Sovereign would remain the same...
still.
And in a time to come,
when the sum of all the kingdom's sin
would scatter them like sheep
without a shepherd,
a voice would be heard in the desert.
Israel would bleat for one like David,
a shepherd-warrior-king
who would cling after God's own heart,
to heal, unify and save.
"Hosanna!" they'd say
as they made clear the way
this One would come,
the Anointed One
— A King from the Ancient of Days.

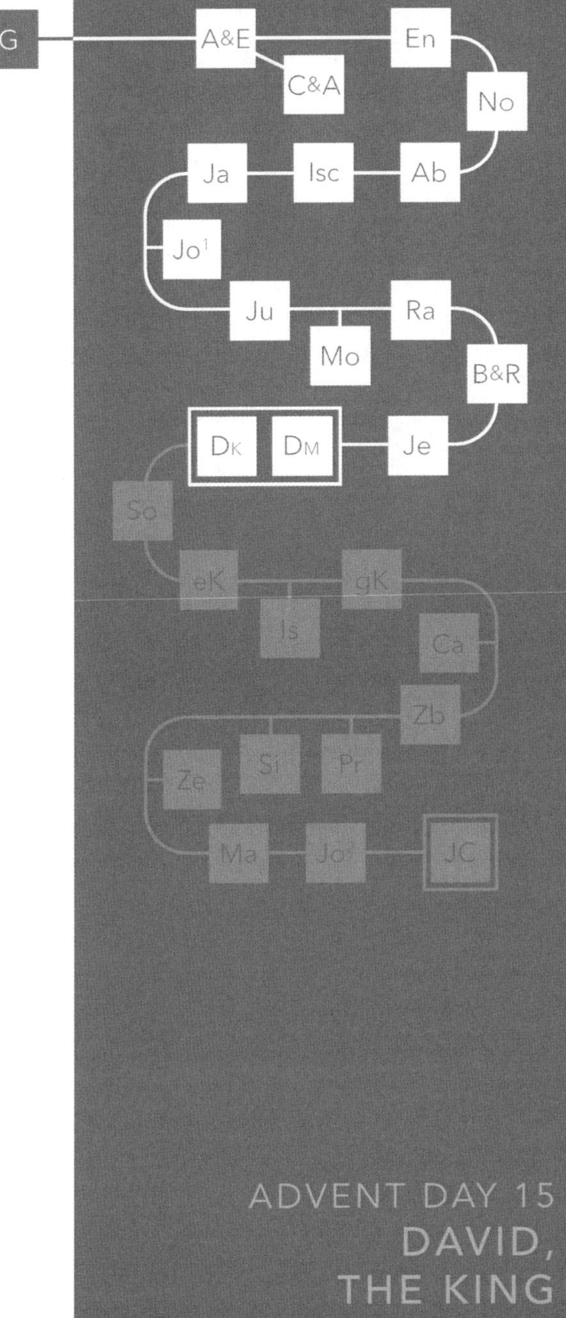

ADVENT DAY 15

DAVID, THE KING

16

SOLOMON

King Solomon excelled all the kings of the earth in riches and in wisdom.

FROM SCRIPTURE, GOD TELLS HIS STORY...

1 KINGS 3:5-9

At Gibeon the Lord appeared to Solomon in a dream by night, and God said, "Ask what I shall give you." And Solomon said, "You have shown great and steadfast love to your servant David my father, because he walked before you in faithfulness, in righteousness, and in uprightness of heart toward you. And you have kept for him this great and steadfast love and have given him a son to sit on his throne this day. And now, O Lord my God, you have made your servant king in place of David my father, although I am but a little child. I do not know how to go out or come in. And your servant is in the midst of your people whom you have chosen, a great people, too many to be numbered or counted for multitude. Give your servant therefore an understanding mind to govern your people, that I may discern between good and evil, for who is able to govern this your great people?"

1 KINGS 11:1-4

Now King Solomon loved many foreign women ...The Lord had said to the people of Israel, "You shall not enter into marriage with them, neither shall they with you, for surely they will turn away your heart after their gods." Solomon clung to these in love. He had 700 wives, who were princesses, and 300 concubines. And his wives turned away his heart. For when Solomon was old his wives turned away his heart after other gods, and his heart was not wholly true to the Lord his God, as was the heart of David his father.

ECCLESIASTES 12:13-14

The end of the matter; all has been heard. Fear God and keep his commandments, for this is the whole duty of man. For God will bring every deed into judgment, with every secret thing, whether good or evil.

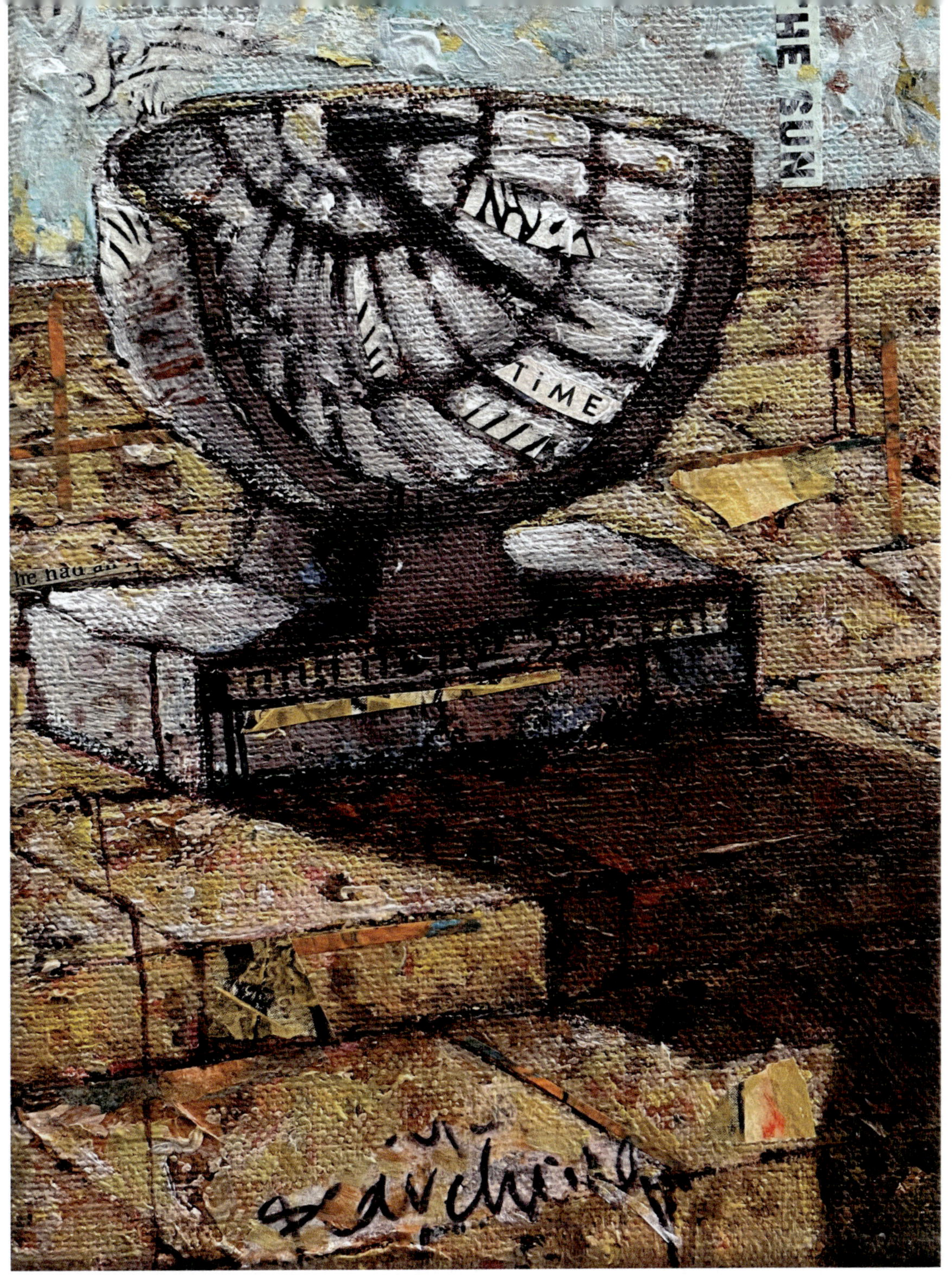
HE SUN
TIME

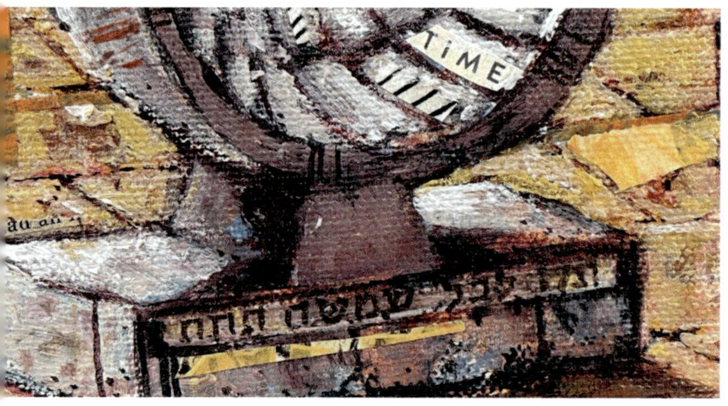

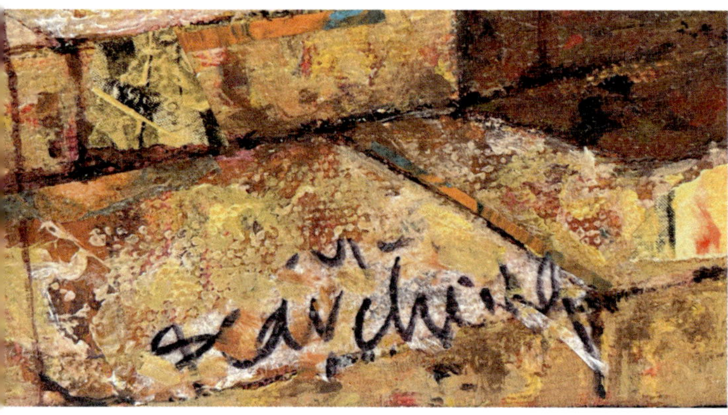

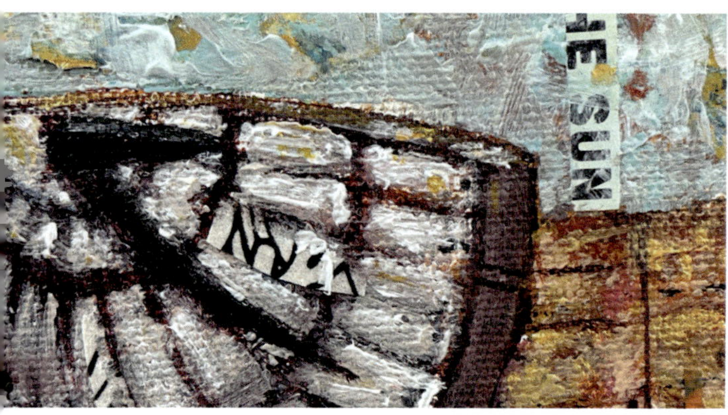

In a sea of subjects we find a boy
afraid of drowning after his crowning
when his father David died.
Solomon cried out to his Lord
who gave him wisdom,
like none before,
to run his kingdom.
"A hearing heart"
right from the start of his reign.
And people came to hear him proclaim
proverbs,
judgments,
and unparalleled reason.
The people would please him
by bringing cedars and gold,
build a house to hold
the presence of the Lord.
A temple to point to Immanuel,
where sacrifice and incense would tell
of One to come.
This was the sum of Israel's Golden Age,
the greatest peace and prosperity
in all its history.
Solomon's splendor
none could compare.
More horses,
more chariots,
more clout.

More wealth,
more women,
and as it turned out,
they would turn him.
A shadow cast as time passed
on the glory of the king.
He applied his heart to wandering
under the sun.
Left him undone,
unwound.
Vanity found.
Sun up to sun down,
it could all spoil
— knowledge, pleasure, and toil.
The wise king acted the fool.
It was a vain thing to do.
For everything,
a season,
and a time for reason
when the folly hidden in shadow
comes to light.
The Preacher would insist,
"The end of the matter is this:
Fear God,
Keep His commands.
This is the enduring joy of man."

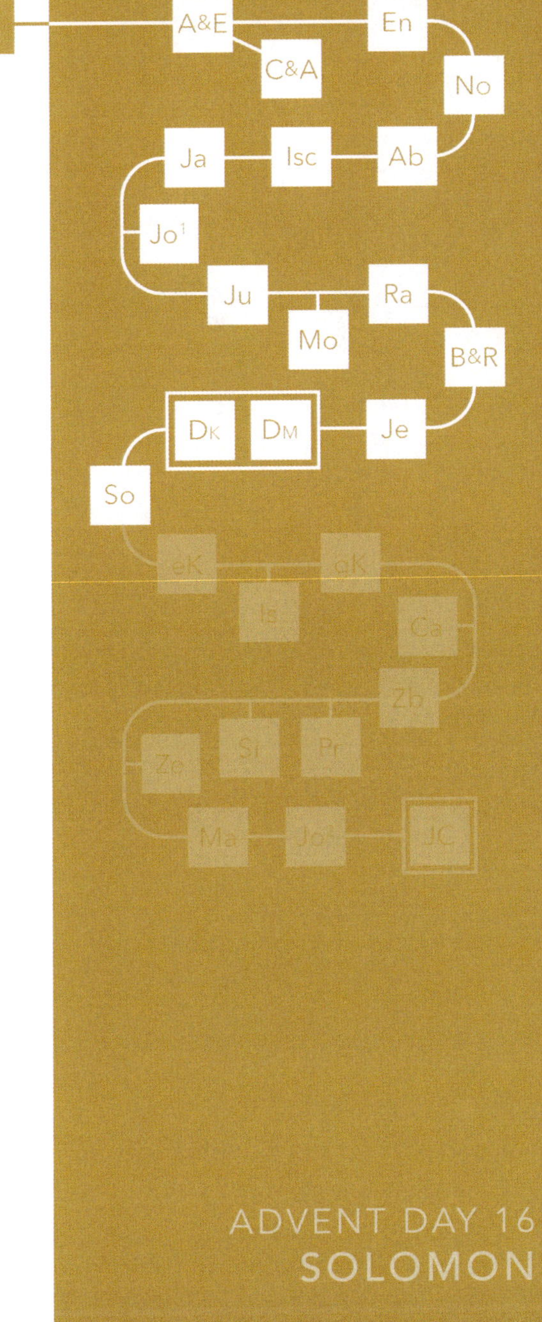

ADVENT DAY 16
SOLOMON

17
EVIL KINGS

He did what was evil in the sight of the LORD and did not humble himself.

FROM SCRIPTURE, GOD TELLS HIS STORY...

DEUTERONOMY 30:15-19

"See, I have set before you today life and good, death and evil. If you obey the commandments of the Lord your God that I command you today, by loving the Lord your God, by walking in his ways, and by keeping his commandments and his statutes and his rules, then you shall live and multiply, and the Lord your God will bless you in the land that you are entering to take possession of it. But if your heart turns away, and you will not hear, but are drawn away to worship other gods and serve them, I declare to you today, that you shall surely perish. You shall not live long in the land that you are going over the Jordan to enter and possess.
I call heaven and earth to witness against you today, that I have set before you life and death, blessing and curse. Therefore choose life, that you and your offspring may live.

2 CHRONICLES 12:14

And [King Rehoboam] did evil, for he did not set his heart to seek the Lord.

EVIL KINGS OF JUDAH

Rehoboam (1 Kings 11:43-14:31)
Abijah (1 Kings 14:31-15:8)
Jehoram or Joram (2 Kings 8:16-24)
Ahaziah (2 Kings 8:24-29; 9:14-28)
Queen Athaliah (2 Kings 11:1-20)
Ahaz (2 Kings 15:38-16:20)
Manasseh (2 Kings 21:1-18)
Amon (2 Kings 21:18-26)
Jehoahaz or Joahaz (2 Kings 23:30-34)
Jehoiakim or Eliakim (2 Kings 23:34-24:6)
Jehoiachin or Coniah or Jeconiah (2 Kings 24:6-17)
Zedekiah or Mattaniah (2 Kings 24:17-25:30)

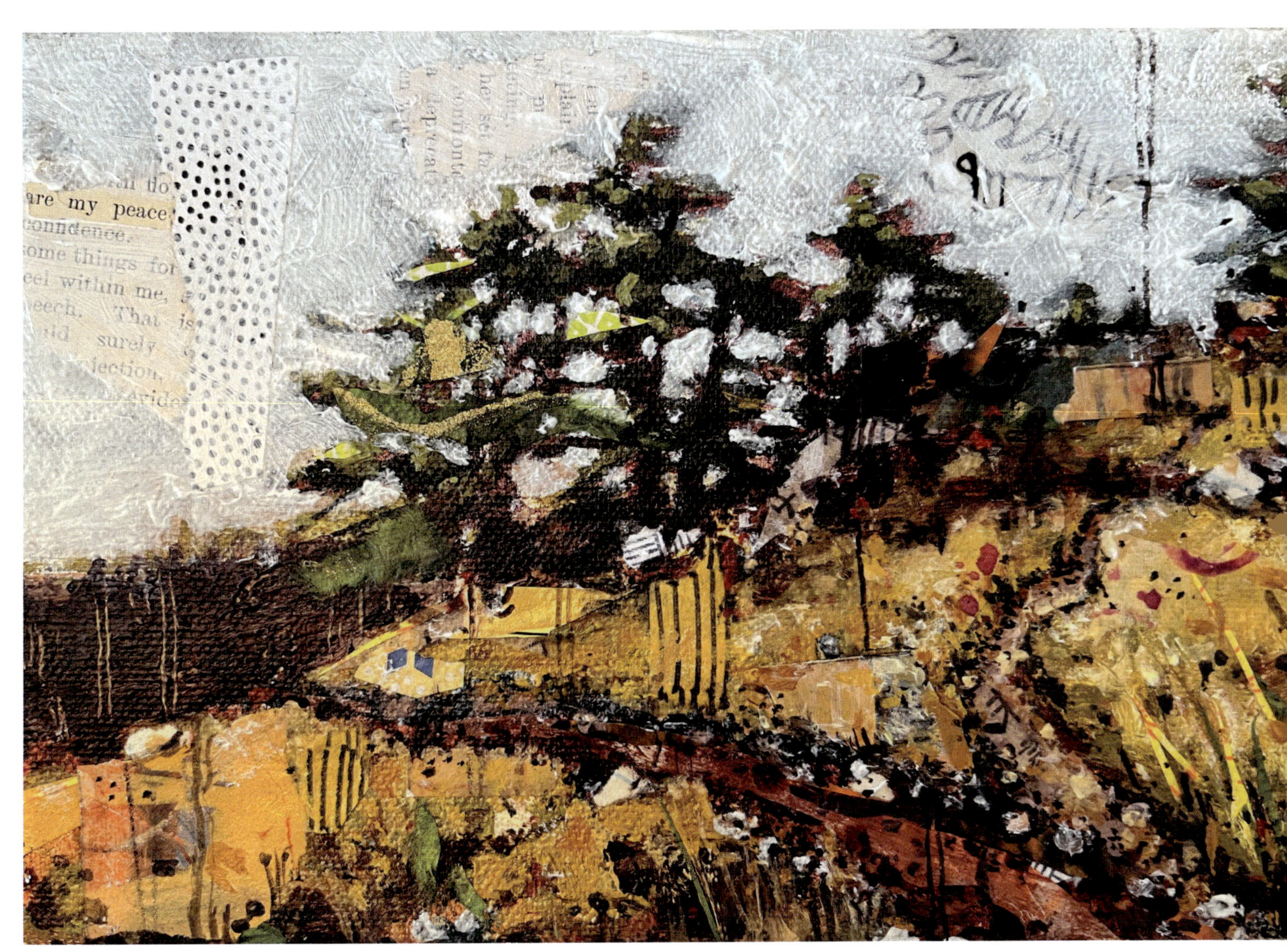
are my peace

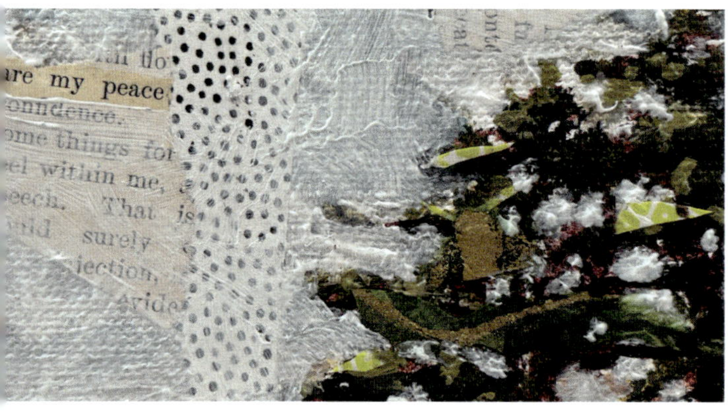

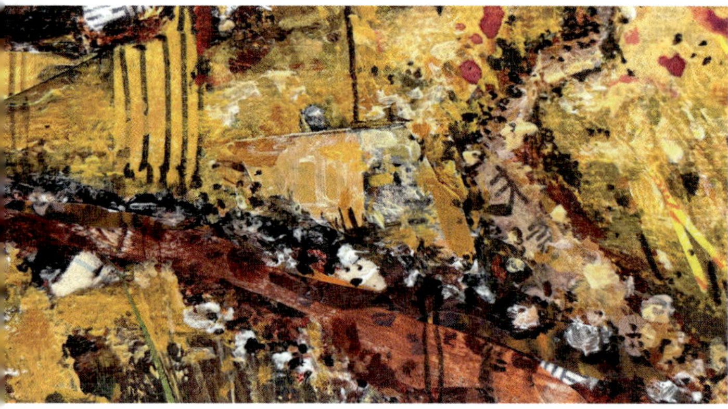

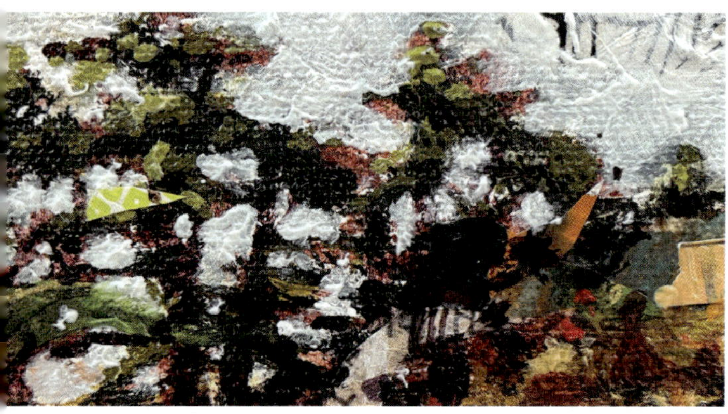

Solomon's son inherited a kingdom shifting,
they were drifting.
Maintaining wealth had cost them.
Israel's health was teetering on the edge.
Continuous building had driven a wedge
into their foundation
— a crack in the nation.
They needed relief.
Rehoboam believed the key
was heavy taxing and increased labor.
God's favor he could spare.
He didn't care.
The burden would break them in two.
A divorce.
Judah in the South
and Israel's kingdom to the North.
They would turn
and bind themselves to evil things.
Two different kings to lead them astray.
And they would pay more than before
because they would ignore
the One who loved them first.
Israel's tribes had once looked over the land
on which they now stood,
and Moses had pointed out two paths,
plain as day.
"Everyone will say to take the way
that seems wide and easy and set,
and yet that will lead to death.

A curse will bring unrest.
But another way, harder I think,
will cause you to cling to One
who can bring you safely through,
blessing you beyond what *you* can do.
That way leads to life."
And Moses was right.
It all came true.
After Israel's split,
seeds of disobedience were sown.
Most kings walked on their own
in the ways of their fathers,
the wide path,
like the others,
riddled with idols and high places,
burning sons,
murdering brothers,
desecrating the temple and others,
in order to appease gods
that could not speak nor hear,
playing the harlot against the God who was near.
The wide path was taken by a string of kings
mocking the Light,
hostile to Him.
How could God begin
to save people like them?
Lovers of sin
again and again.

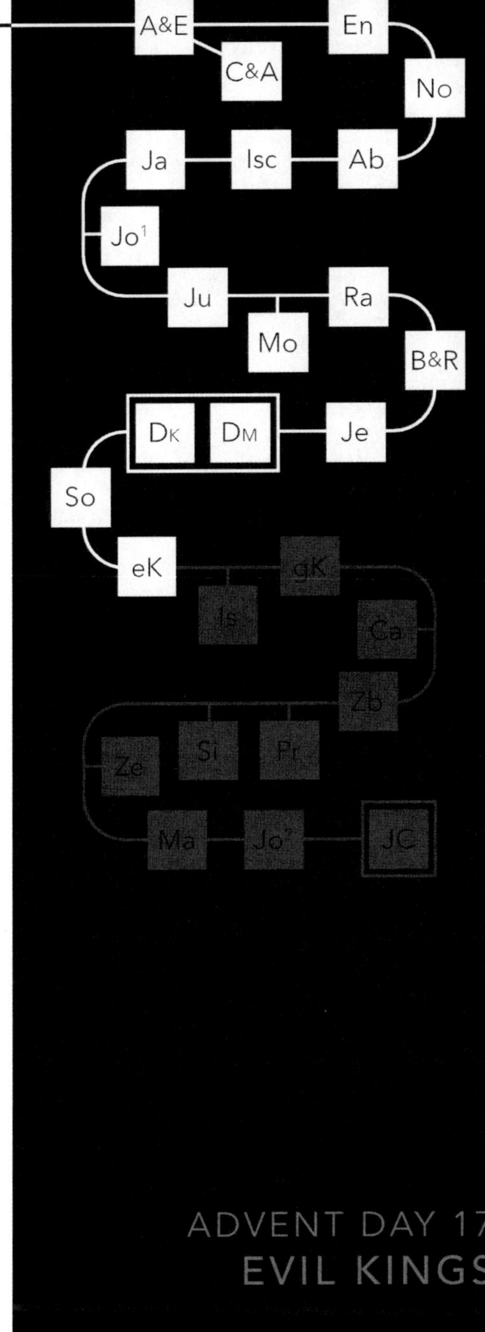

18

ISAIAH

My eyes have seen

the King,

the Lord of Hosts!

FROM SCRIPTURE, GOD TELLS HIS STORY...

ISAIAH 6:1

In the year that King Uzziah died I saw the Lord sitting upon a throne, high and lifted up; and the train of his robe filled the temple.

Isaiah's vision (Isaiah 6:2-4)

ISAIAH 6:5-8

And [Isaiah] said: "Woe is me! For I am lost; for I am a man of unclean lips, and I dwell in the midst of a people of unclean lips; for my eyes have seen the King, the Lord of hosts!"

Then one of the seraphim flew to me, having in his hand a burning coal that he had taken with tongs from the altar. And he touched my mouth and said: "Behold, this has touched your lips; your guilt is taken away, and your sin atoned for."

And I heard the voice of the Lord saying, "Whom shall I send, and who will go for us?" Then I said, "Here I am! Send me."

ISAIAH 9:2,6

The people who walked in darkness have seen a great light; those who dwelt in a land of deep darkness, on them has light shone.
... For to us a child is born, to us a son is given; and the government shall be upon his shoulder, and his name shall be called Wonderful Counselor, Mighty God, Everlasting Father, Prince of Peace.

LUKE 4:17-21

And the scroll of the prophet Isaiah was given to [Jesus]. He unrolled the scroll and found the place where it was written,

"The Spirit of the Lord is upon me, because he has anointed me to proclaim good news to the poor. He has sent me to proclaim liberty to the captives and recovering of sight to the blind, to set at liberty those who are oppressed, to proclaim the year of the Lord's favor."

And he rolled up the scroll and gave it back to the attendant and sat down. And the eyes of all in the synagogue were fixed on him. And he began to say to them, "Today this Scripture has been fulfilled in your hearing."

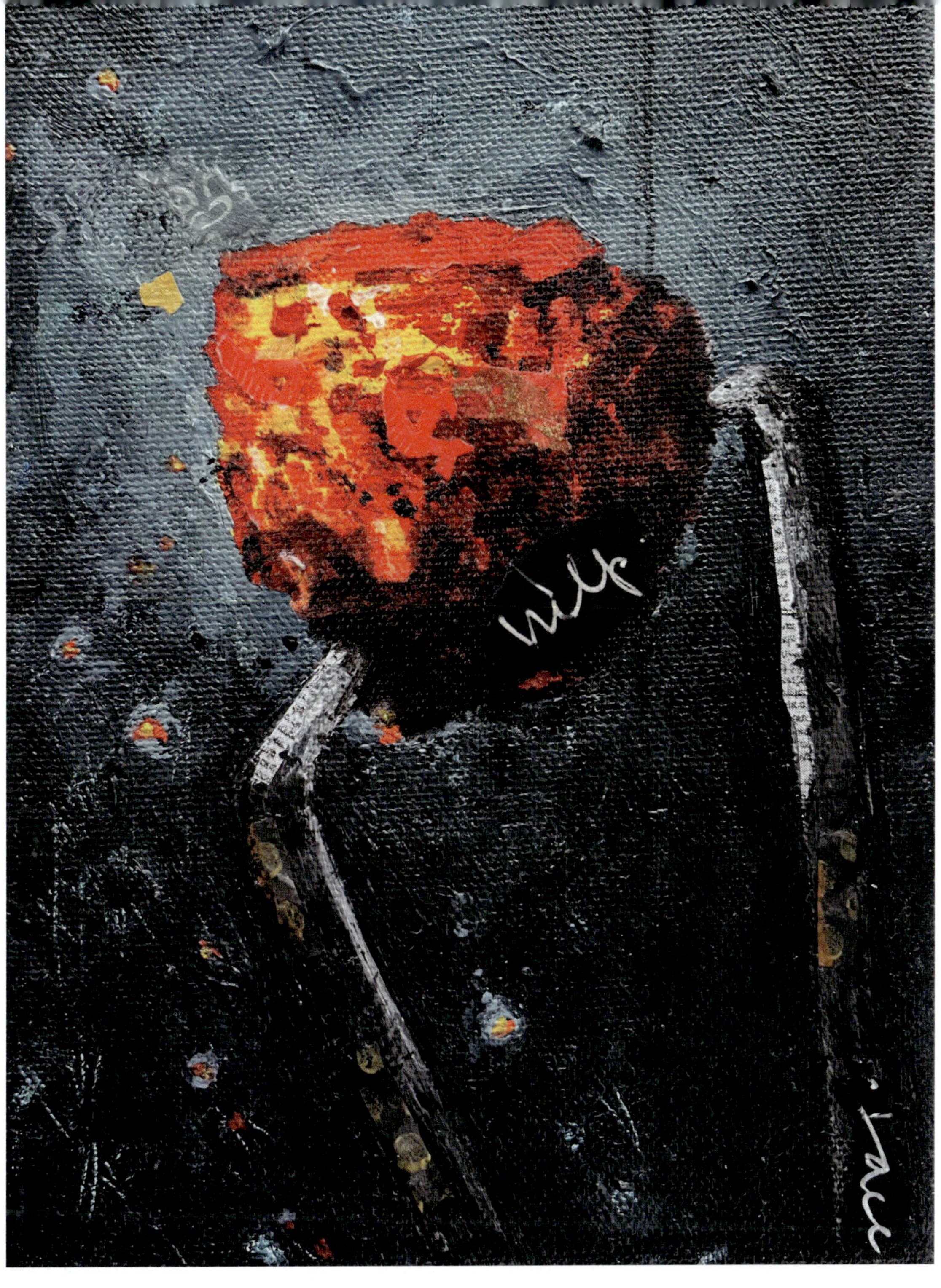

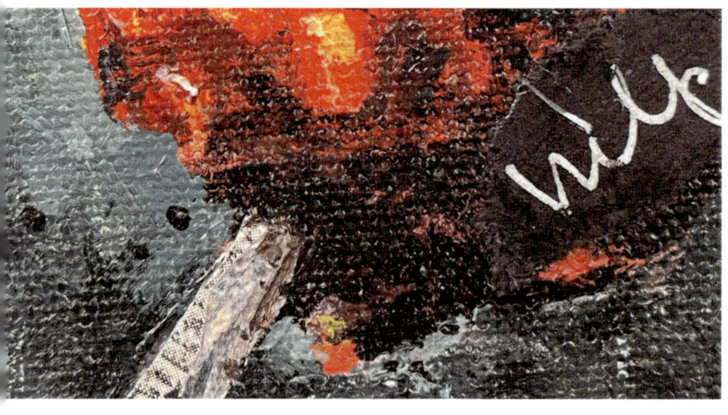

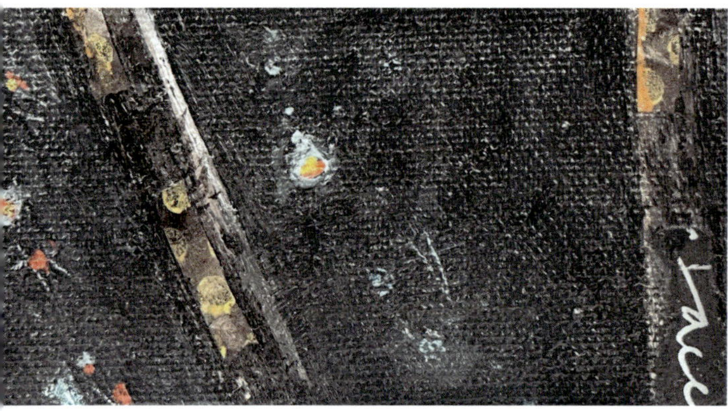

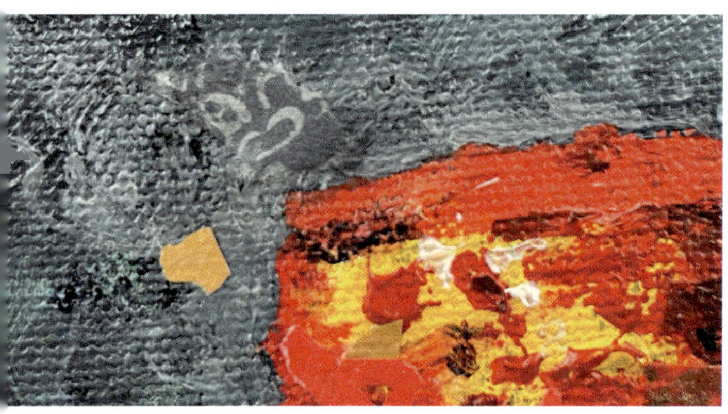

King Uzziah was gone.
But the kings on the throne
were never the one promised
who would shepherd like David.
None had risen.

A prophet.
A vision.
In the throne room of a king,
but none Isaiah had ever seen or known.
The One on the throne,
his robe and glory filled the place.
Profoundly made aware of the chasm
between who he was and who he saw.
Undone by fear and awe.
A Judge, severe and right.
Isaiah, condemned in His sight.
Woe, woe, woe.
"Woe is me!
I am unclean!
My eyes have seen the King of Kings!"

From the altar where sacrifice was made
and sin was paid,
a burning coal was carried
and placed on his trembling mouth.
The unholy was refined
by the Holy, Holy, Holy.

Isaiah wholly forgiven
in light of the darkness he lived in.
His Sovereign would send him
to those who walked in darkness
and defamed His name.
Affliction would test before rest could come.
It would seem as though the serpent had won,
but the Son would rise.
Isaiah would describe this great light
so the people could see with their own eyes
the King to come
— the Wonderful Counselor,
Mighty God and Everlasting One,
this Prince of Peace.

After centuries of darkness and scorn
a child would be born,
and the world would be torn in two.
All that the prophet said was true.
A man would stand with a scroll in His hand
and open to where Isaiah had penned,
"The Spirit of the Lord is upon me
and anointed me to preach good news to the poor;
to set captives free."
And if you could see
the surprise in their eyes as to who this could be,
this humble shoot from Jesse's tree.
Holy is He.

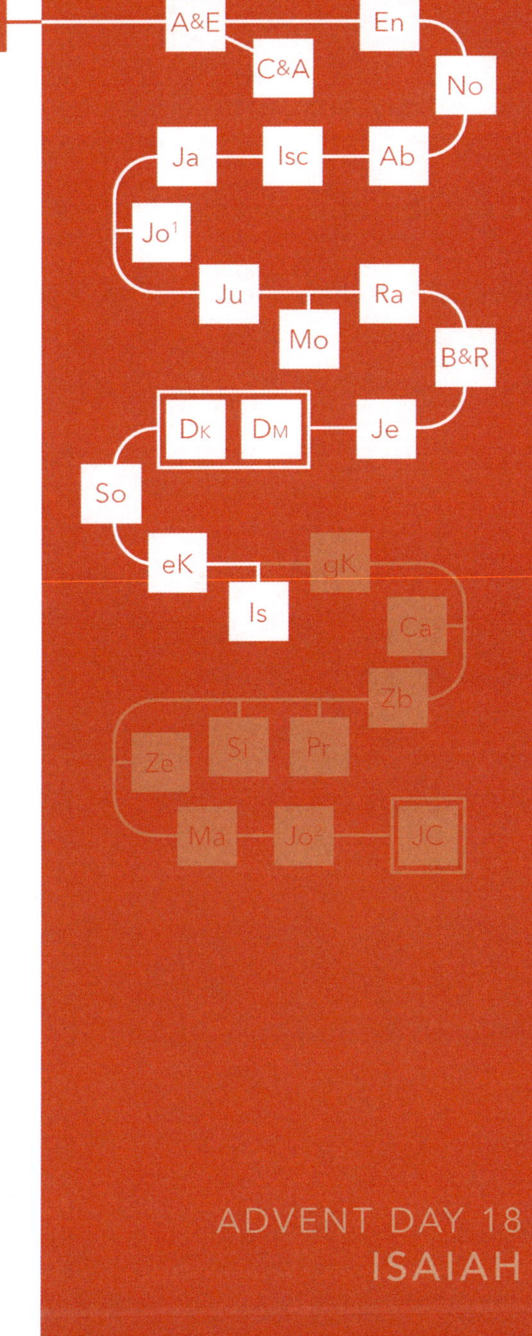

ADVENT DAY 18
ISAIAH

19

GOOD KINGS

...That he may learn to fear the Lord his God by keeping all the words of this law.

FROM SCRIPTURE, GOD TELLS HIS STORY...

2 CHRONICLES 17:3-6

The Lord was with [King] Jehoshaphat, because he walked in the earlier ways of his father David. He did not seek the Baals, but sought the God of his father and walked in his commandments, and not according to the practices of Israel. Therefore the Lord established the kingdom in his hand. And all Judah brought tribute to Jehoshaphat, and he had great riches and honor. His heart was courageous in the ways of the Lord. And furthermore, he took the high places and the Asherim out of Judah.

2 KINGS 23:2-3, 25

And [King Josiah] went up to the house of the Lord, and with him all the men of Judah and all the inhabitants of Jerusalem and the priests and the prophets, all the people, both small and great. And he read in their hearing all the words of the Book of the Covenant that had been found in the house of the Lord. And the king stood by the pillar and made a covenant before the Lord, to walk after the Lord and to keep his commandments and his testimonies and his statutes with all his heart and all his soul, to perform the words of this covenant that were written in this book. And all the people joined in the covenant.

... Before [Josiah] there was no king like him, who turned to the Lord with all his heart and with all his soul and with all his might, according to all the Law of Moses, nor did any like him arise after him.

GOOD KINGS OF JUDAH

Asa or Asaph (1 Kings 15:8-24)
Jehoshaphat (1 Kings 15:24; 22:1-50)
Joash or Jehoash (2 Kings 11:1-12:21)
Amaziah (2 Kings 14:1-22)
Uzziah or Azariah, in the beginning of his reign (2 Kings 15:1-7)
Jotham (2 Kings 15:32-38)
Hezekiah (2 Kings 16:20, 18:1-20:21)
Josiah (2 Kings 21:26-23:30)

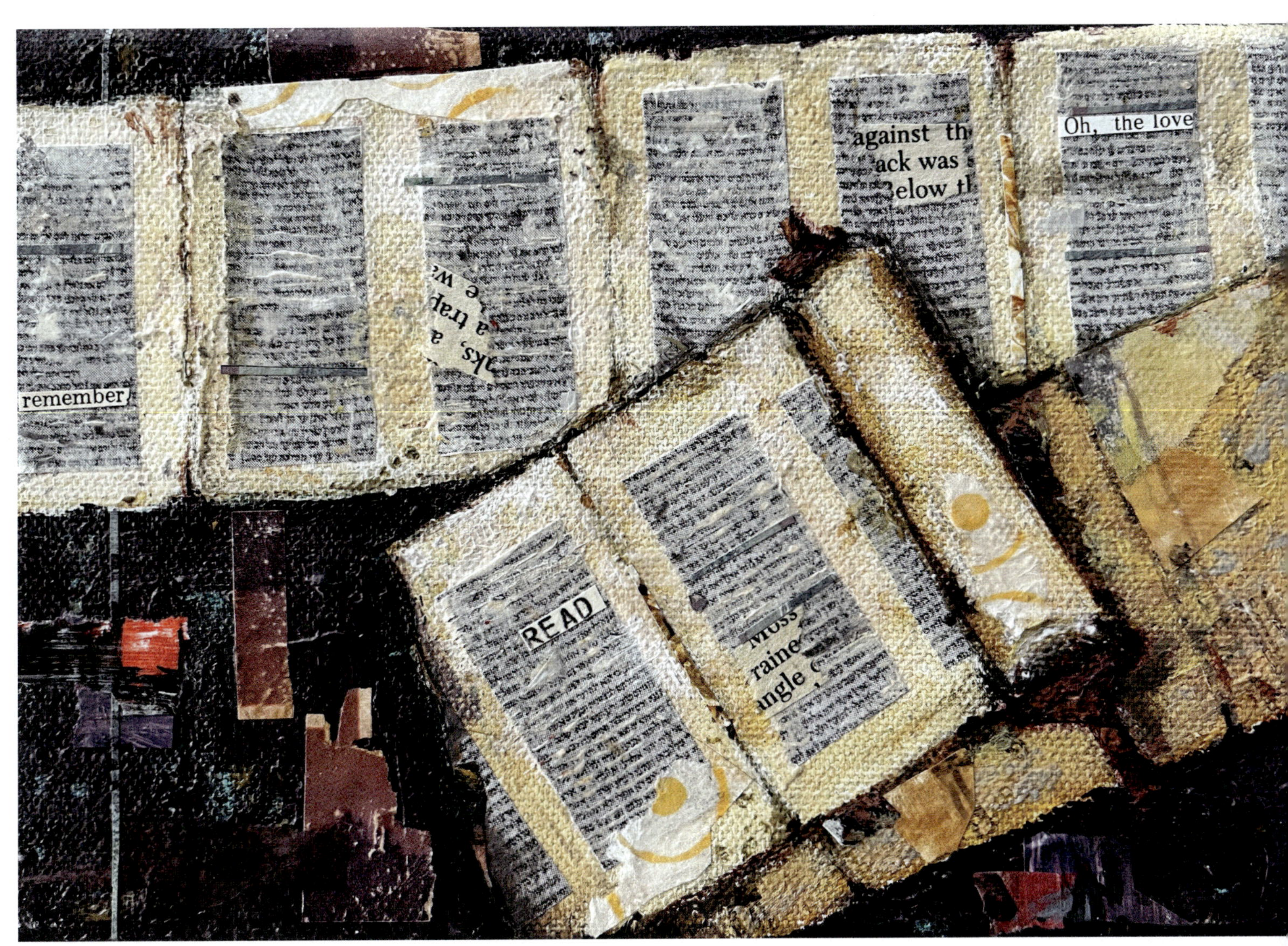
remember
Oh, the love
against th
ack was
READ
Moss
raine
angle

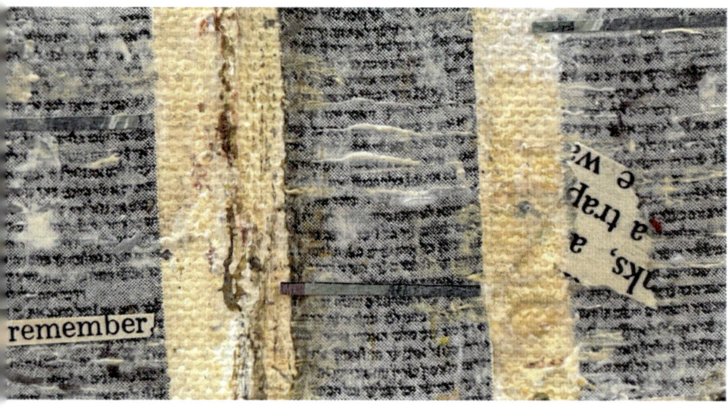

Israel, the kingdom in the North, was so far gone.
Prophets with warnings and signs had come,
but they killed the messengers instead.
Led away by an Assyrian king.
Judah, the kingdom in the South, still stood,
because in a string of evil kings
there were rare glimpses of light.
A king would fight to turn right
when his father had left the way.
And God would stay His hand
until again the people,
like sheep, would stray.

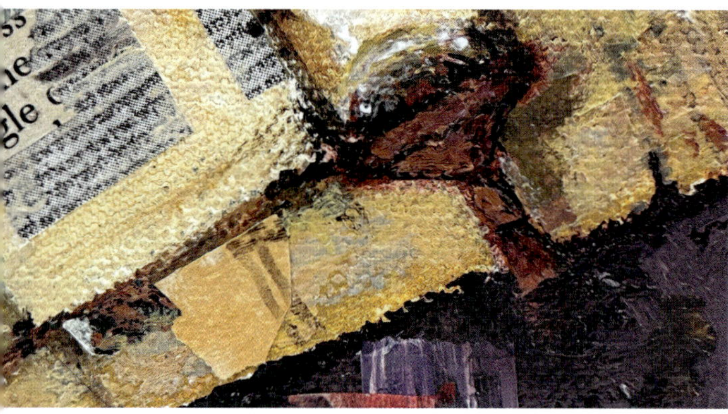

King Asa was wholly devoted to the Lord
all his days and in mighty ways
would bring honor back.
King Jehoshaphat taught from the Law.
And when he saw the enemy near,
would fear,
but in front of all would call out to his Lord.
"We do not know what to do,
but our eyes are on You."
And the army watched God fight that day.

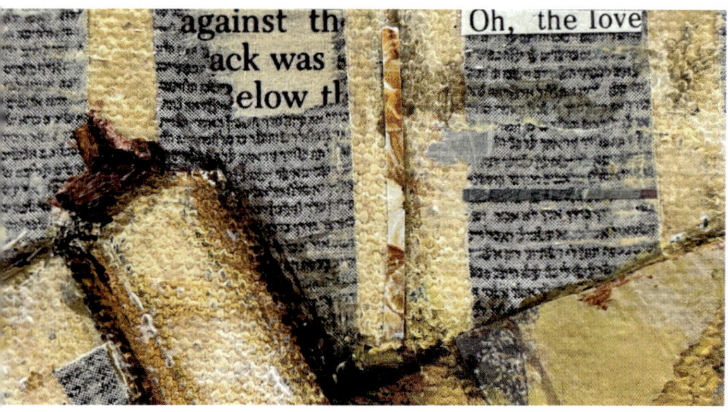

King Jehoash and Amaziah,
Jotham and Hezekiah,
they would all walk in the way of David,
after God's own heart.
But the nation would soon part
when those kings died.

God's honor, erased. The temple disgraced.
High places were scattered as false waypoints all about.
Their flame nearly snuffed out.
But young Josiah was a light.
His reign began in the darkest of night,
evil at its height,
but he would not turn to the left
nor to the right off the path.
The idols all around, he chopped them up,
pulled them down, burned them to the ground.
And when his men worked to restore
the house of the Lord,
scrolls were found,
pulled from the heap,
brought to the king and read.
When Josiah heard what it said he tore his clothes.
God's words made it plain how far they strayed.
A covenant was made for the rest of his days
with the Author of the Law.
They would not fall.
Josiah would do everything written in the book,
no matter what it took.
Blessing would rest on the kings who carried the light,
who did what was right,
but it wouldn't last.
Night would come fast. Allegiance done.
A nightmare would come to wake them.
A new enemy would take them.

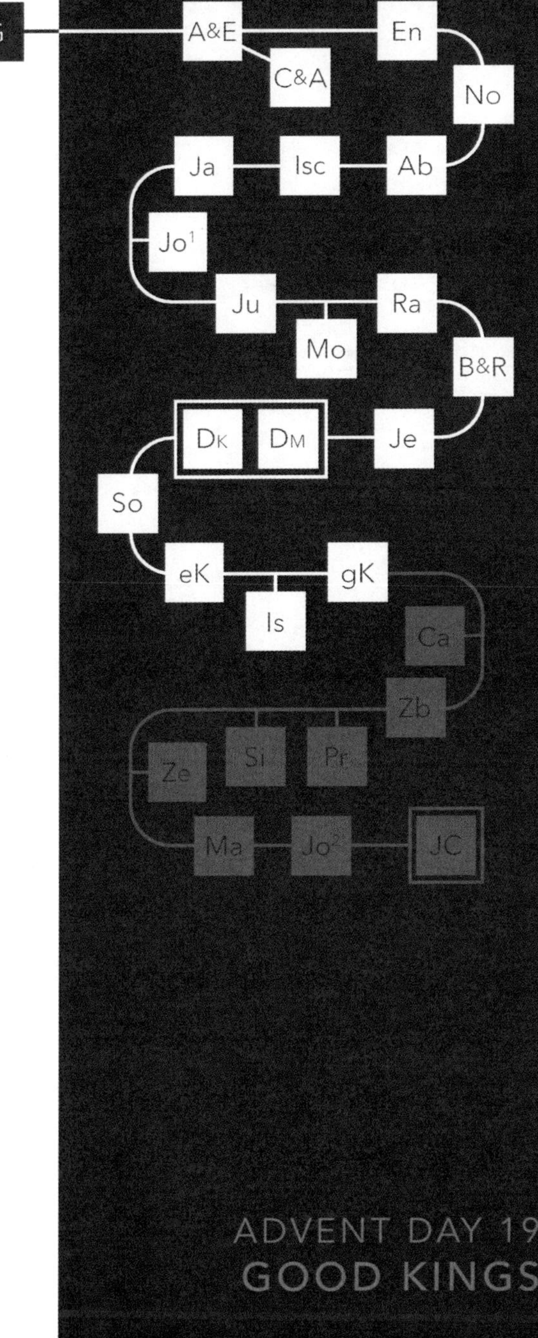

ADVENT DAY 19
GOOD KINGS

20

CAPTIVITY

O daughter of
Jerusalem,
your ruin is vast;
who can heal you?

FROM SCRIPTURE, GOD TELLS HIS STORY...

2 KINGS 24:10-15

At that time the servants of Nebuchadnezzar king of Babylon came up to Jerusalem, and the city was besieged. And Nebuchadnezzar king of Babylon came to the city while his servants were besieging it, and Jehoiachin the king of Judah gave himself up to the king of Babylon, himself and his mother and his servants and his officials and his palace officials. The king of Babylon took him prisoner in the eighth year of his reign and carried off all the treasures of the house of the Lord and the treasures of the king's house, and cut in pieces all the vessels of gold in the temple of the Lord, which Solomon king of Israel had made, as the Lord had foretold. He carried away all Jerusalem and all the officials and all the mighty men of valor, 10,000 captives, and all the craftsmen and the smiths. None remained, except the poorest people of the land. And he carried away Jehoiachin to Babylon.

2 KINGS 25:8-9

... In the nineteenth year of King Nebuchadnezzar, king of Babylon—Nebuzaradan, the captain of the bodyguard, a servant of the king of Babylon, came to Jerusalem. And he burned the house of the Lord and the king's house and all the houses of Jerusalem; every great house he burned down.

A kingdom undone (2 Kings 25:10-30)
The undoing explained (Jeremiah 25:8-12)
God's plan (Jeremiah 29:1-14)

MATTHEW 23:37-39

"O Jerusalem, Jerusalem, the city that kills the prophets and stones those who are sent to it! How often would I have gathered your children together as a hen gathers her brood under her wings, and you were not willing! See, your house is left to you desolate. For I tell you, you will not see me again, until you say, 'Blessed is he who comes in the name of the Lord.'"

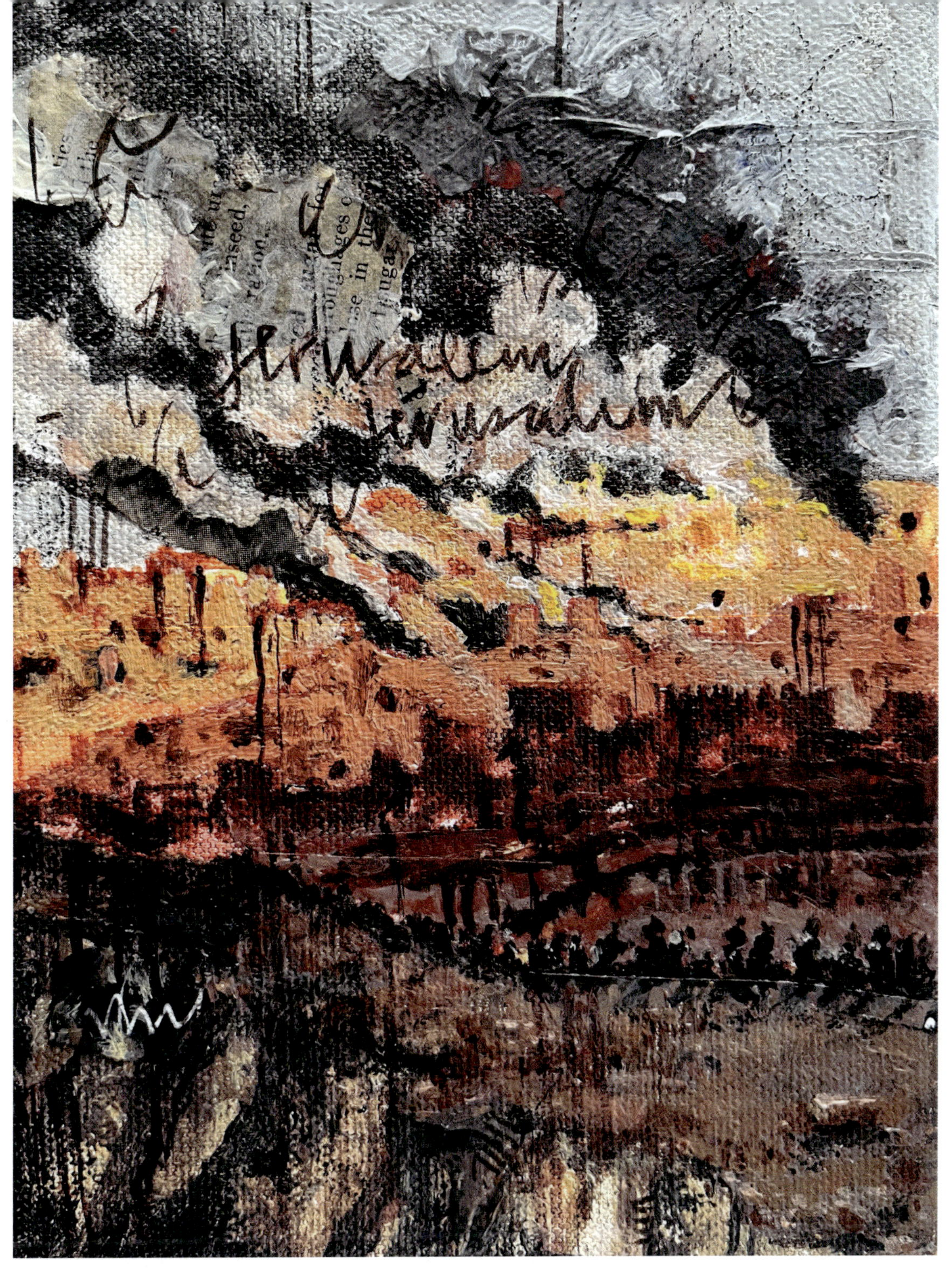
Jerusalem

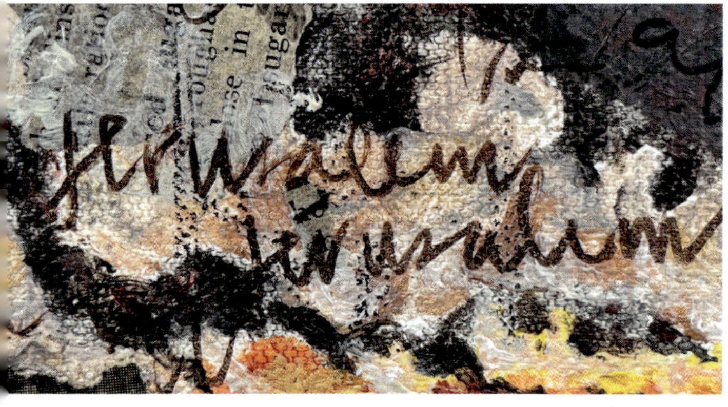

Josiah's son led the kingdom back into sin.
Then, Egypt again, would oppress
and Babylon would heavily press its control too
until it pushed through.
Three seiges of Jerusalem began.
The Lord would send Nebuchadnezzar
to take His prodigal children away.
The delivered
would become slaves again,
carrying a heap of sins upon their backs
and God's anger would rest
like a foot upon their necks...
like His foe.
O Jerusalem, Jerusalem,
the city that killed the prophets He sent,
how much He longed to cover you
under His wings,
but you'd have none of it.
The ashes of woe would cover
the beautiful city of David.
Stripped bare.
The nations would stare at her shame.
Mothers moaning,
holding lifeless children.
Men, aimlessly walking, talking.
Noone listening.
The temple glistening in flames.
Destruction unmeasured.

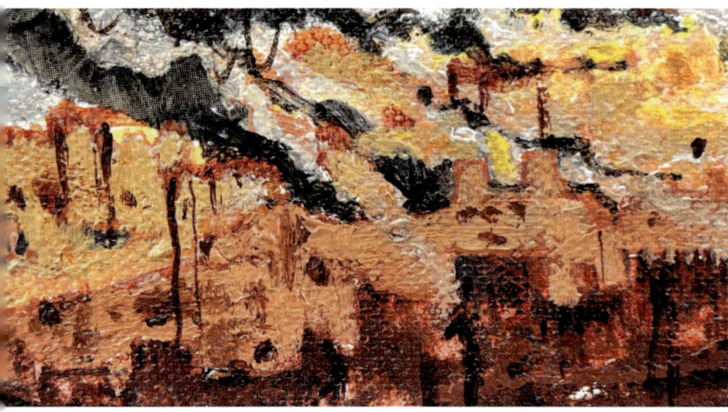

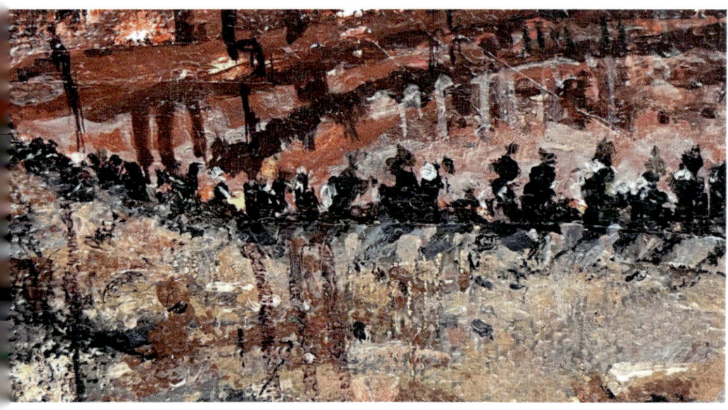

Judah's king was added to the Babylonian treasures.
His people led away in chains,
carried away on that lamentable day.
Daniel, Hananiah, Mishael, and Azariah,
Jeremiah, Ezekiel, Mordicai.
The weeping prophet would cry;
the Lord would proclaim,
"I have sent you into exile;
I have done all these things.
After you've groaned and grown
in the place you land;
I will bring you back.
For you, I have plans.
You will call to me
and I will hear.
You'll seek Me again
and find Me near."
It is good for all those who wait on Him.
The Father will not reject forever.
In lovingkindness, He will send a Savior.
Yearn for Him.
Examine and learn.
Return.

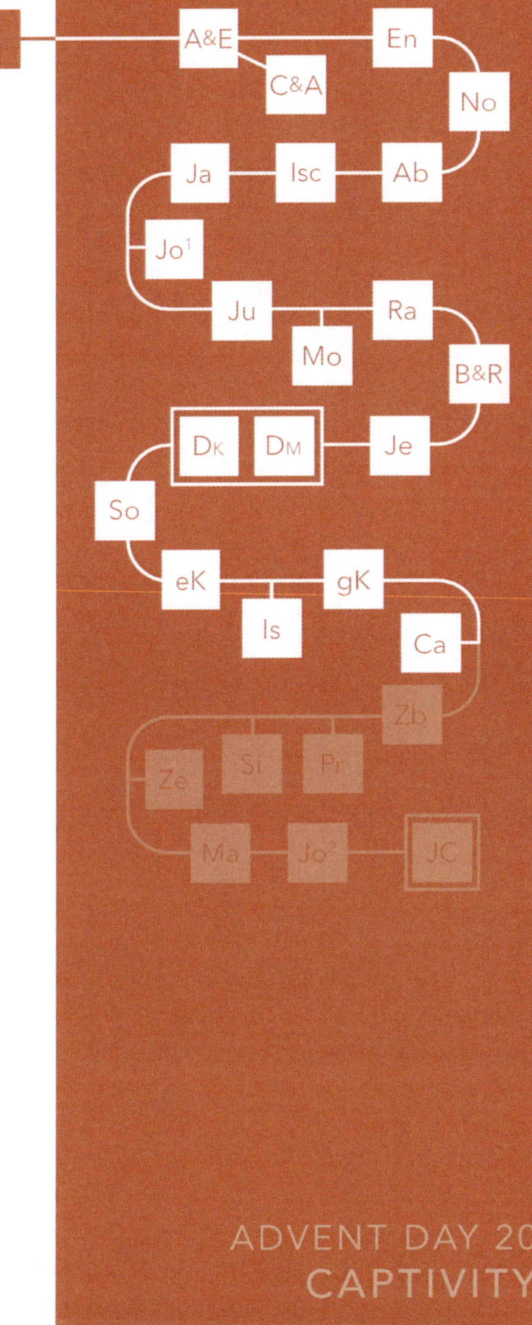

ADVENT DAY 20
CAPTIVITY

21

ZERUBBABEL

I will make you

like a signet ring,

for I have

chosen you.

FROM SCRIPTURE, GOD TELLS HIS STORY...

MATTHEW 1:12

And after the deportation to Babylon: Jechoniah was the father of Shealtiel, and Shealtiel the father of Zerubbabel.

JEREMIAH 22:24
(regarding the last of the evil kings of Judah, Zerubbabel's grandfather)
"As I live, declares the LORD, though [Jechoniah] the son of Jehoiakim, king of Judah, were the signet ring on my right hand, yet I would tear you off."

God moves the heart of a Persian king (Ezra 1:1-4)

HAGGAI 2:1-5, 21-23

The word of the Lord came by the hand of Haggai the prophet: "Speak now to Zerubbabel the son of Shealtiel, governor of Judah, and to Joshua the son of Jehozadak, the high priest, and to all the remnant of the people, and say, 'Who is left among you who saw this house in its former glory? How do you see it now? Is it not as nothing in your eyes? Yet now be strong, O Zerubbabel, declares the Lord. Be strong, O Joshua, son of Jehozadak, the high priest. Be strong, all you people of the land, declares the Lord. Work, for I am with you, declares the Lord of hosts, according to the covenant that I made with you when you came out of Egypt. My Spirit remains in your midst. Fear not.

... I am about to shake the heavens and the earth, and to overthrow the throne of kingdoms ... On that day, declares the Lord of hosts, I will take you, O Zerubbabel my servant, the son of Shealtiel, declares the Lord, and make you like a signet ring, for I have chosen you, declares the Lord of hosts."

ZECHARIAH 4:6-10

Then he said to me, "This is the word of the Lord to Zerubbabel: Not by might, nor by power, but by my Spirit, says the Lord of hosts. Who are you, O great mountain? Before Zerubbabel you shall become a plain. And he shall bring forward the top stone amid shouts of 'Grace, grace to it!'

...The hands of Zerubbabel have laid the foundation of this house; his hands shall also complete it. Then you will know that the Lord of hosts has sent me to you. For whoever has despised the day of small things shall rejoice, and shall see the plumb line in the hand of Zerubbabel."

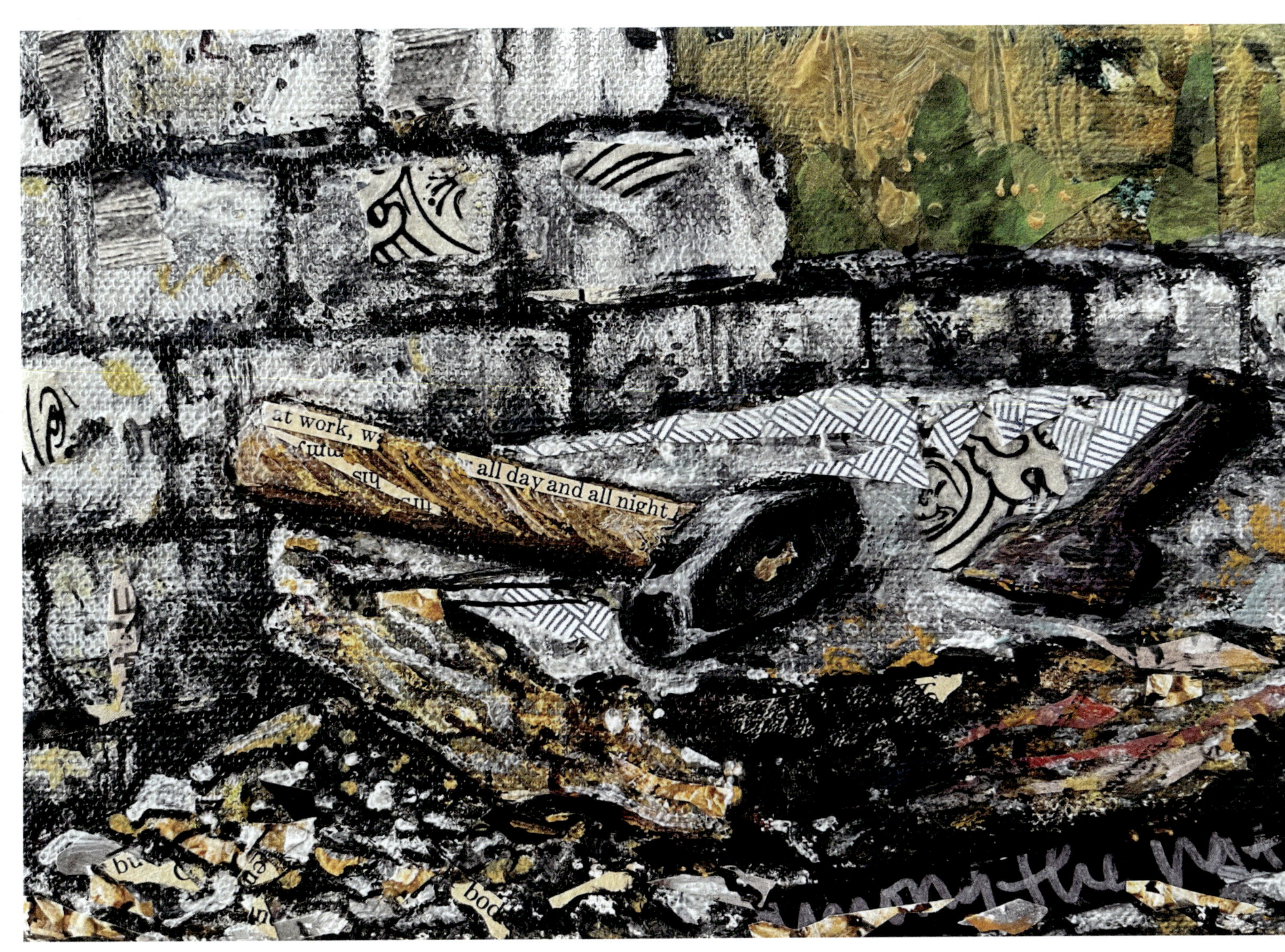
at work,
all day and all night

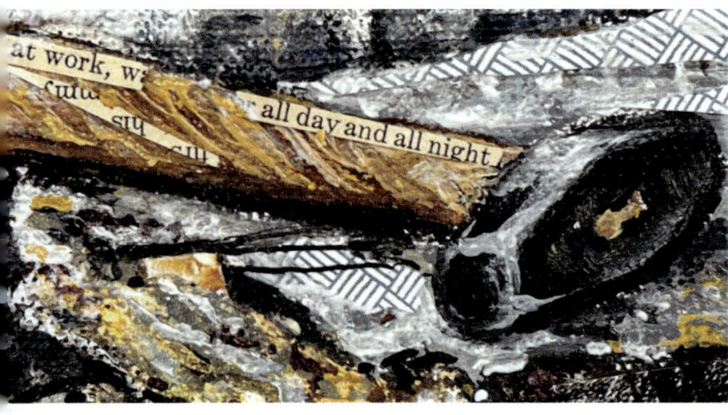

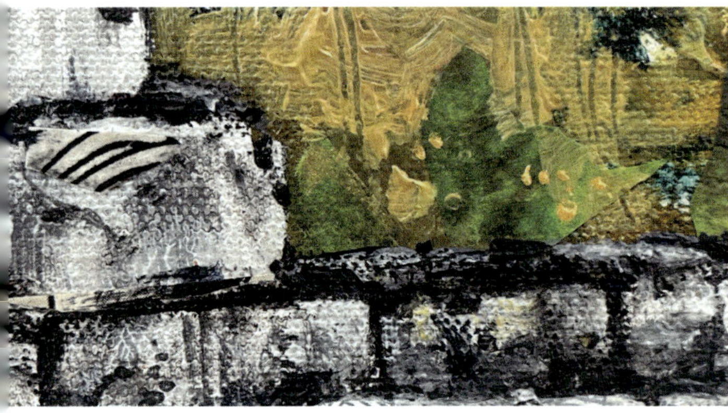

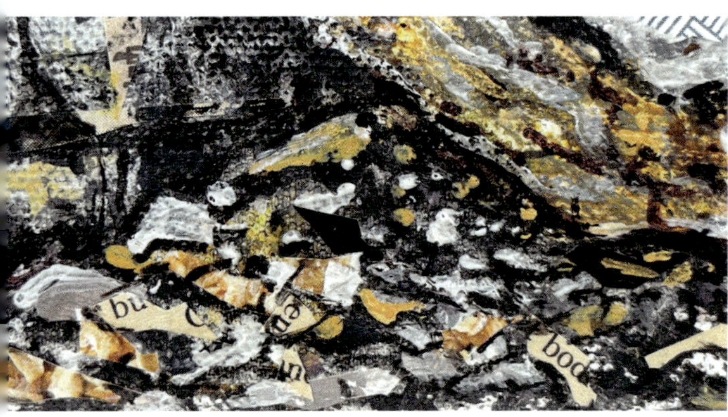

Jerusalem tattered, Israel scattered.
Persia ruling now.
Shamed for the name they carried
among people who buried that flame.
A new generation came, born in captivity too.
This was all they knew.
But God would move the heart of Cyrus, the king.
A decree would grant freedom
for the Jews of the land
to rebuild Jerusalem and the temple again.
One man in the snuffed out royal line,
Zerubbabel
— the son of Shealtiel,
the son of the last evil king
who was stripped of God's favor —
this son born in exile would lead the endeavor.
The Lord would speak to Zerubbael,
Babylon's seed,
"I removed your fathers from the kingly line.
They served another.
They were not Mine.
But I choose you,
despite your name, from whence you came,
or what the curse demands.
I place you like a signet ring on my right hand.
All you need is at My command.
Your success is sure.
Because, my son, all I have is now yours."

Stone by stone,
piece by piece,
they would build.
Zerubbabel would hold the plumb line still.
And year after year they would yield
to the sure foundation
beneath their feet and fear.
The articles taken, the scrolls forsaken,
the gold and silver, and all the tools needed
were given until they at last succeeded
and all the nations could see a light
again on that holy hill.
A broken place restored greater than its former glory.
Zerubbabel's story
is the story of all who belong to Him.
Born into sin.
Babylon's seed within.
Impossible to change my name.
But an adoption takes place.
A display of His grace.
The Father says, "You are mine,"
though nothing I bring.
Once an enemy,
now an heir to a King.
All that is His He yields to me.
All I need to rebuild the temple He filled
He brings.
This is my story. This is the song I sing.

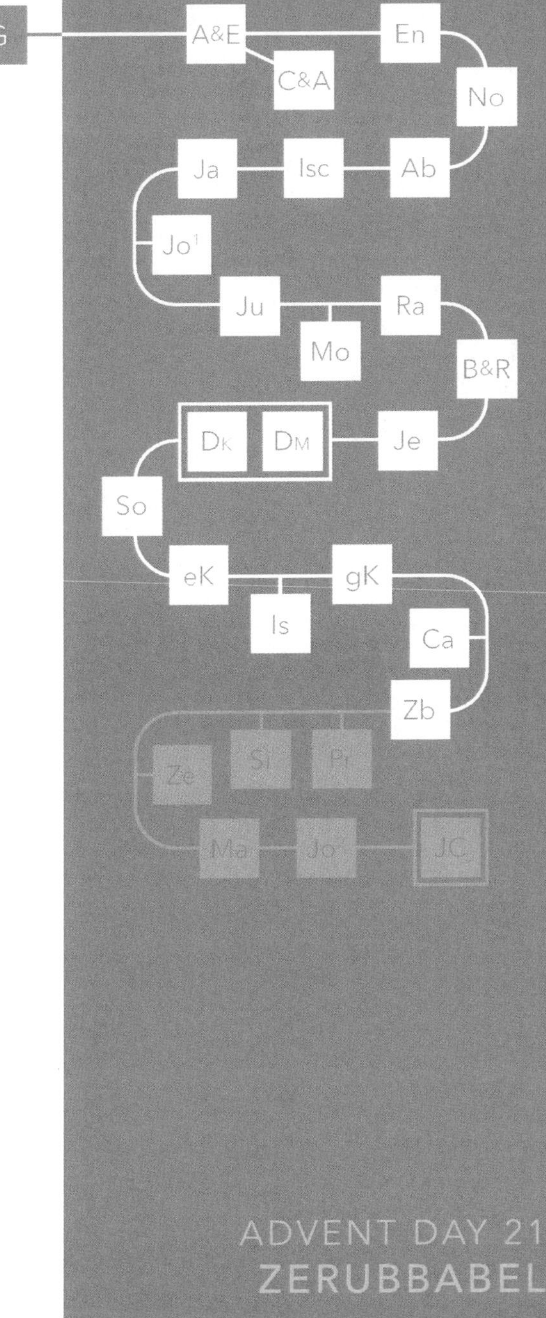

ADVENT DAY 21
ZERUBBABEL

22

PROPHECY

We have found him of whom Moses in the Law and also the prophets wrote.

FROM SCRIPTURE, GOD TELLS HIS STORY...

(These prophecies were all spoken and recorded centuries before Jesus was born.)

MICAH 5:2

But you, O Bethlehem Ephrathah, who are too little to be among the clans of Judah, from you shall come forth for me one who is to be ruler in Israel, whose coming forth is from of old, from ancient days.

The seed of Eve (Genesis 3:14-15)
God promises Abraham (Genesis 12:3; 28:13-14)
Judah's sceptor (Genesis 49:10)

HOSEA 11:1

When Israel was a child, I loved him, and out of Egypt I called my son.

A prepared way (Malachi 3:1)
A shoot from a stump (Isaiah 11:1; Jeremiah 23:5-6)
A forever king (2 Samuel 7:12-13)

ISAIAH 7:14

Therefore the Lord himself will give you a sign. Behold, the virgin shall conceive and bear a son, and shall call his name Immanuel.

Kings bring gifts (Psalm 72:10-11; Matthew 2:1-11)

ZECHARIAH 9:9

Rejoice greatly, O daughter of Zion! Shout aloud, O daughter of Jerusalem! Behold, your king is coming to you; righteous and having salvation is he, humble and mounted on a donkey, on a colt, the foal of a donkey.

Betrayed by a friend (Psalm 41:9; 55:12-14)
A rejected stone (Psalm 118:22-23; Isaiah 8:14-15)
A humiliated king (Psalm 22)
Suffering servant (Isaiah 52:13-53:12)

ZECHARIAH 12:10

And I will pour out on the house of David and the inhabitants of Jerusalem a spirit of grace and pleas for mercy, so that, when they look on me, on him whom they have pierced, they shall mourn for him.

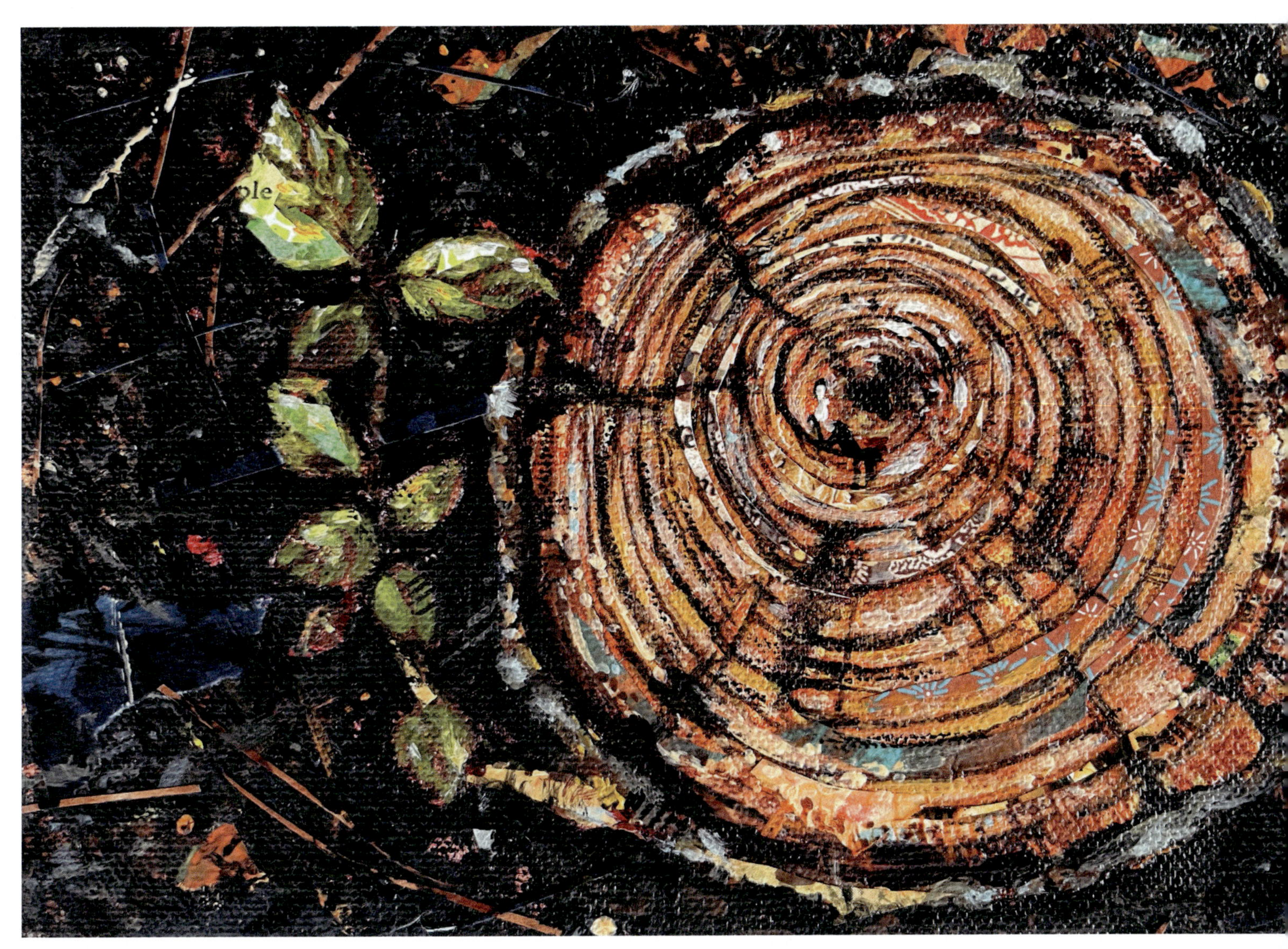

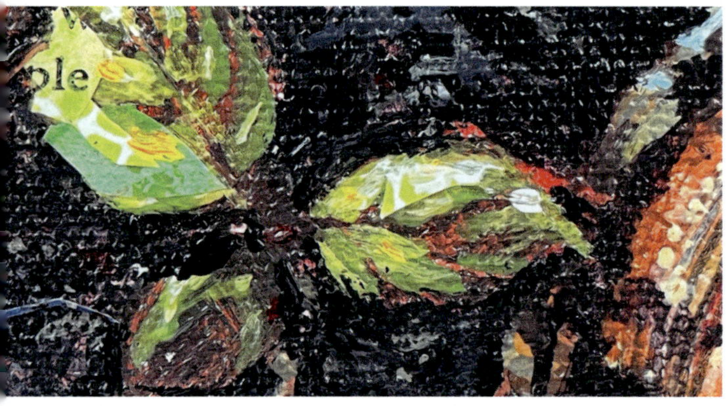

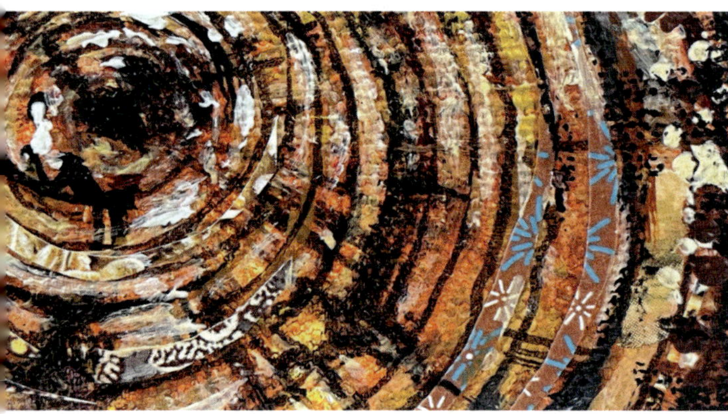

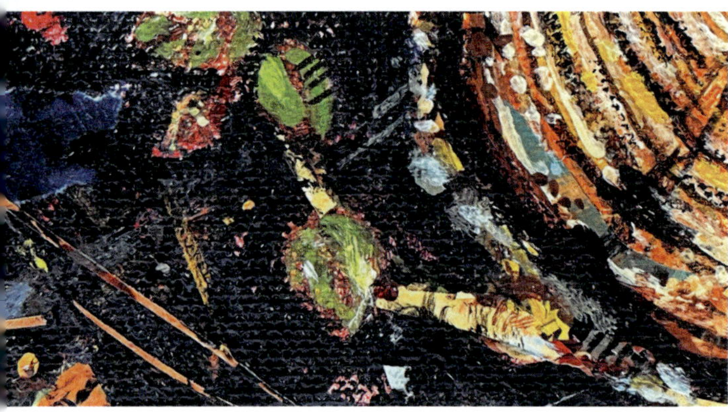

In the beginning, the Word.
He planted revelation in creation.
Seed from Eve would crush, though bruised.
From among weeds, God would choose Abraham.
Through his seed all the nations would be blessed,
and a test would foreshadow its cost.
The loss of a son.
Jacob perceived the scepter
would not leave Judah's branch,
until the true King came.
A lion would reign.
A shoot would come from Jesse's stem.
Prophecy extending.
God tending the line from David's throne
that would grow forever.
Just like him,
one would come from Bethlehem,
small and unseen.
Foreign kings would bring gifts to see this child
born to a virgin girl.
The world would shift at the chosen One.
God's begotten son,
out of Egypt, would come.
A messenger would prepare eyes to recognize
the one despised and rejected by men.
He'd enter Jerusalem on a donkey.
The perfect one would enter a lowly way.
Humble. Bruised.

His close friend would betray,
but the Messiah would stay silent,
like a lamb to the slaughter.
Our filthy sins would fall on Him.
The pure one would pay a guilt offering.
And it would satisfy the Father
that His Son would die
in place of the ones He loved.
His cover divided at the foot of a tree.
He'd cry, "Why have you forsaken me?"

Every word spoken and written
centuries before a star ever shone.
The prophets would unveil
birth, life, death, even his name
so we would know him when he came.
Prophecy.
Different rings in a tree, connection unseen.
As the tree would grow, only the bark would show
the signs of the times.
How could the King reign if He was to die?
How could a kingdom endure if it was to fall?
But when the Son fell,
the rings in that old rugged tree
would tell the story of how a seed in the garden
grew to its full glory.
And how we'd been told all along
the One who was, and is, and is to come.

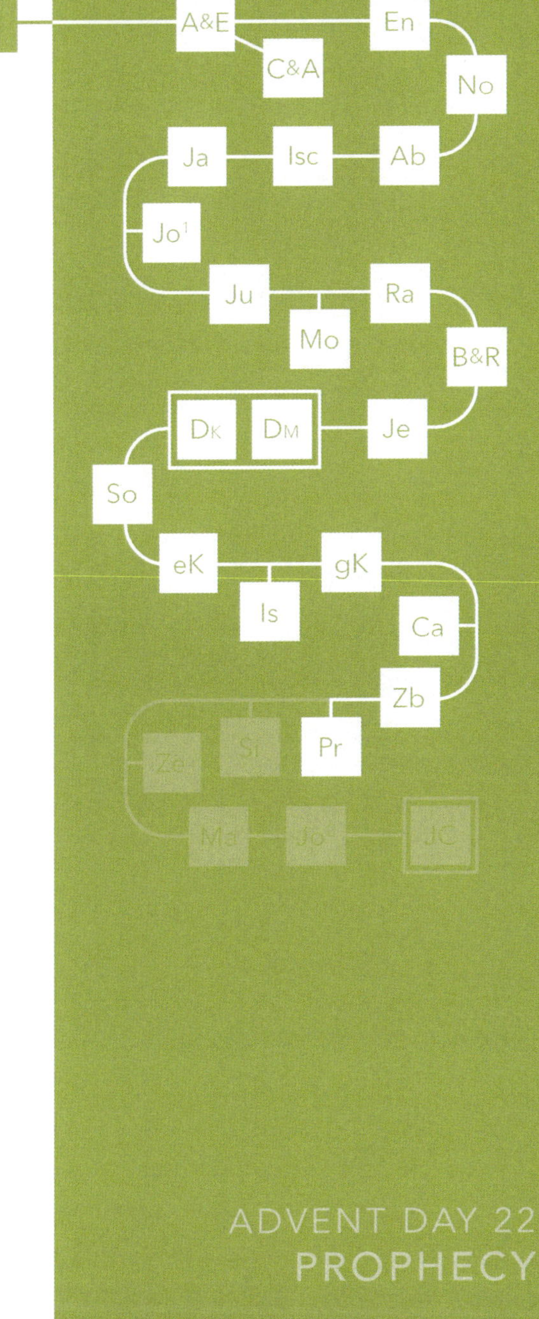

ADVENT DAY 22
PROPHECY

23

SILENCE

Wait in silence,

for my hope

is from Him.

FROM SCRIPTURE, GOD TELLS HIS STORY...

(The word selah, included in many of the Psalms, is understood to be a technical musical term indicating a transition, a musical suspension, or a pause. It seems to be intentionally placed for the purpose of reflecting on what has just been sung in the lyrics.)

PSALM 44:1-2,8-9,23-26

O God, we have heard with our ears, our fathers have told us, what deeds you performed in their days, in the days of old: You with your own hand drove out the nations, but them you planted; you afflicted the peoples, but them you set free.

... In God we have boasted continually, and we will give thanks to your name forever. *Selah*
But you have rejected us and disgraced us and have not gone out with our armies.

... Awake! Why are you sleeping, O Lord? Rouse yourself! Do not reject us forever! Why do you hide your face? Why do you forget our affliction and oppression? For our soul is bowed down to the dust; our belly clings to the ground. Rise up; come to our help! Redeem us for the sake of your steadfast love!

PSALM 62:5

For God alone, O my soul, wait in silence, for my hope is from him.

MALACHI 3:13-18

"Your words have been hard against me," says the Lord.

But you say, "How have we spoken against you?"

You have said, "It is vain to serve God. What is the profit of our keeping his charge or of walking as in mourning before the Lord of hosts? And now we call the arrogant blessed. Evildoers not only prosper but they put God to the test and they escape."

Then those who feared the Lord spoke with one another. The Lord paid attention and heard them, and a book of remembrance was written before him of those who feared the Lord and esteemed his name.

"They shall be mine," says the Lord of hosts, "in the day when I make up my treasured possession, and I will spare them as a man spares his son who serves him. Then once more you shall see the distinction between the righteous and the wicked, between one who serves God and one who does not serve him."

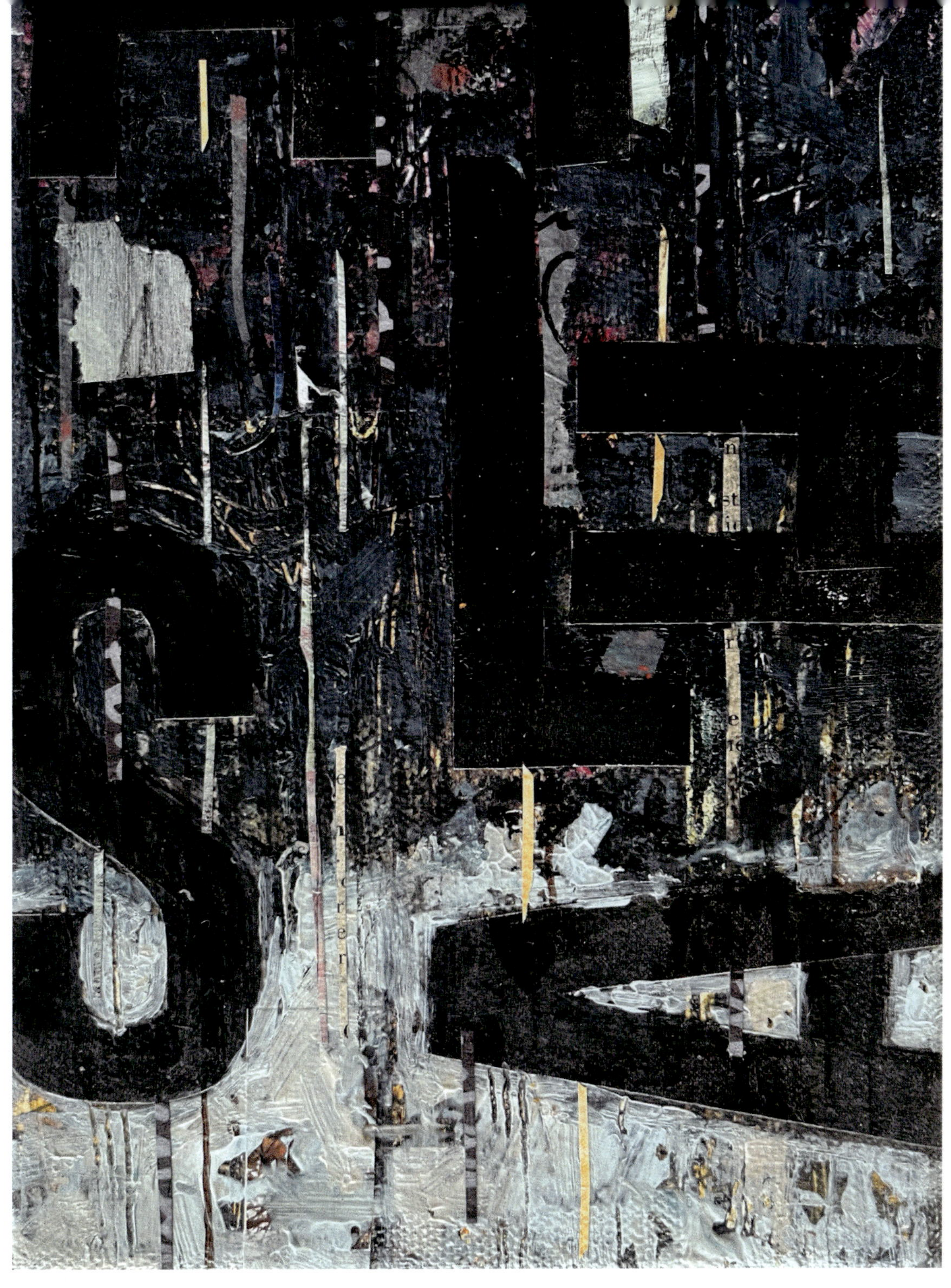

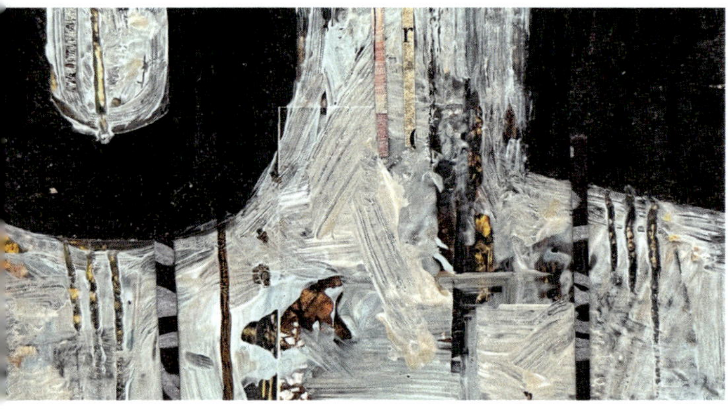

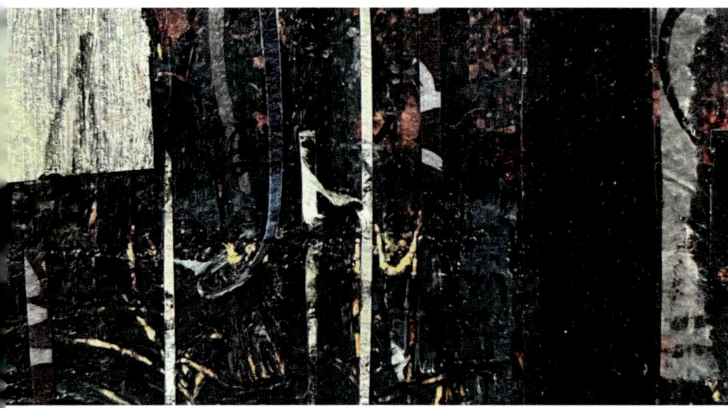

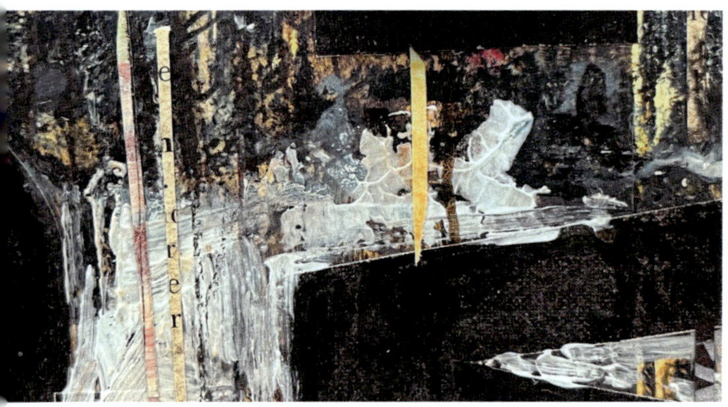

For years upon years
no miracles,
no prophets,
no new word was heard.
God was silent.
A pause was cause for worry.
Surely God relented on the promise
to send One to save
or they had just missed Him
in the day-to-day.
Either way, serving a silent God was foolish.
Babylon, then Persia,
Egypt, Greece, now Rome,
those rulers would come instead.
And what they said was heard loud and clear.
Fear, quite near.
But God's word was…
distant.
Nostalgic at best.
Blurred memories of a former time
when they had signs to feed their faith.
What does it pay a child to obey
if the arrogant are blessed
and the wicked can test the Father
and escape?
Seemed in vain.
A messiah never came.
Selah.

But a remnant remained
who would stop and listen
to what had been written
before.
"I do not change," said the Lord.
So they would gather,
no matter the noise in their ears
and the years of waiting,
with prophecy unfulfilled.
If He said it,
they would not forget it.
Believed His promises were true,
those faithful few.
And a distinction was made in the dark
between those who believed
and those who did not,
between those who filled the void with noise
and thoe who would stop and listen.
Selah.

A long-standing promise was humming,
prophecy was strumming.
400 years of silence was there
to hear Him coming.
Selah.

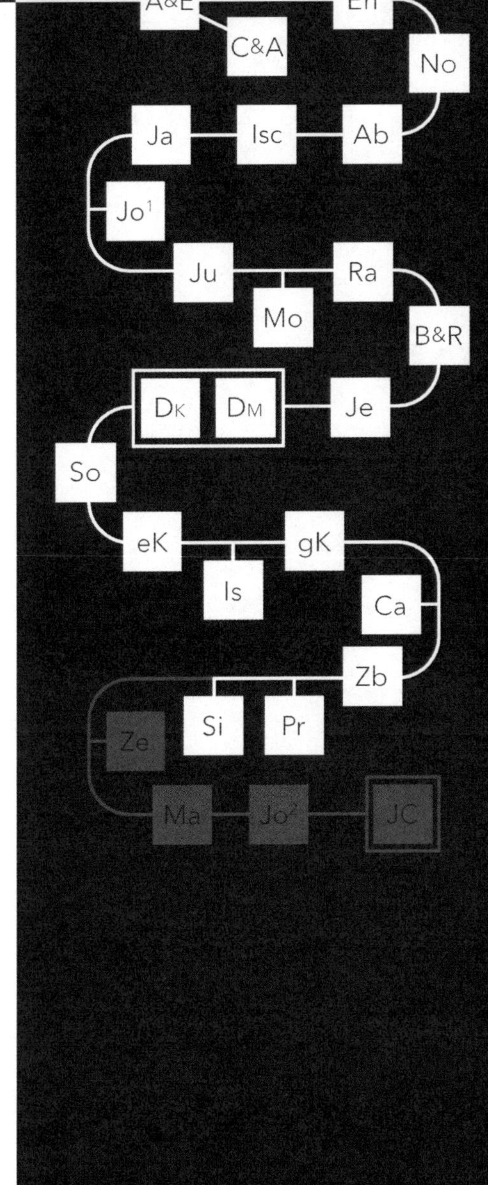

ADVENT DAY 23
SILENCE

24

ZECHARIAH

And you, child,
will go before
the Lord
to prepare His ways.

FROM SCRIPTURE, GOD TELLS HIS STORY...

LUKE 1:5-24, 57-64

In the days of Herod, king of Judea, there was a priest named Zechariah, of the division of Abijah. He had a wife from the daughters of Aaron, and her name was Elizabeth. And they were both righteous before God, walking blamelessly in all the commandments and statutes of the Lord. But they had no child, because Elizabeth was barren, and both were advanced in years.

Now while he was serving as priest before God,... he was chosen by lot to enter the temple of the Lord and burn incense. And the whole multitude of the people were praying outside ... And there appeared to him an angel of the Lord standing on the right side of the altar of incense. And Zechariah was troubled when he saw him, and fear fell upon him. But the angel said to him, "Do not be afraid, Zechariah, for your prayer has been heard, and your wife Elizabeth will bear you a son, and you shall call his name John. And you will have joy and gladness, and many will rejoice at his birth, for he will be great before the Lord ... And he will turn many of the children of Israel to the Lord their God, and he will go before him in the spirit and power of Elijah, to turn the hearts of the fathers to the children, and the disobedient to the wisdom of the just, to make ready for the Lord a people prepared."

And Zechariah said to the angel, "How shall I know this? For I am an old man, and my wife is advanced in years." And the angel answered him, "I am Gabriel. I stand in the presence of God, and I was sent to speak to you and to bring you this good news. And behold, you will be silent and unable to speak until the day that these things take place, because you did not believe my words, which will be fulfilled in their time." ... And when [Zechariah] came out, he was unable to speak to them ... And he kept making signs to them and remained mute.

... After these days his wife Elizabeth conceived.

... Now the time came for Elizabeth to give birth, and she bore a son ... They would have called him Zechariah after his father, but his mother answered, "No; he shall be called John." And they said to her, "None of your relatives is called by this name." And they made signs to his father... And he asked for a writing tablet and wrote, "His name is John." And they all wondered. And immediately his mouth was opened and his tongue loosed, and he spoke, blessing God.

Zechariah prophesies (Luke 1:67-80)

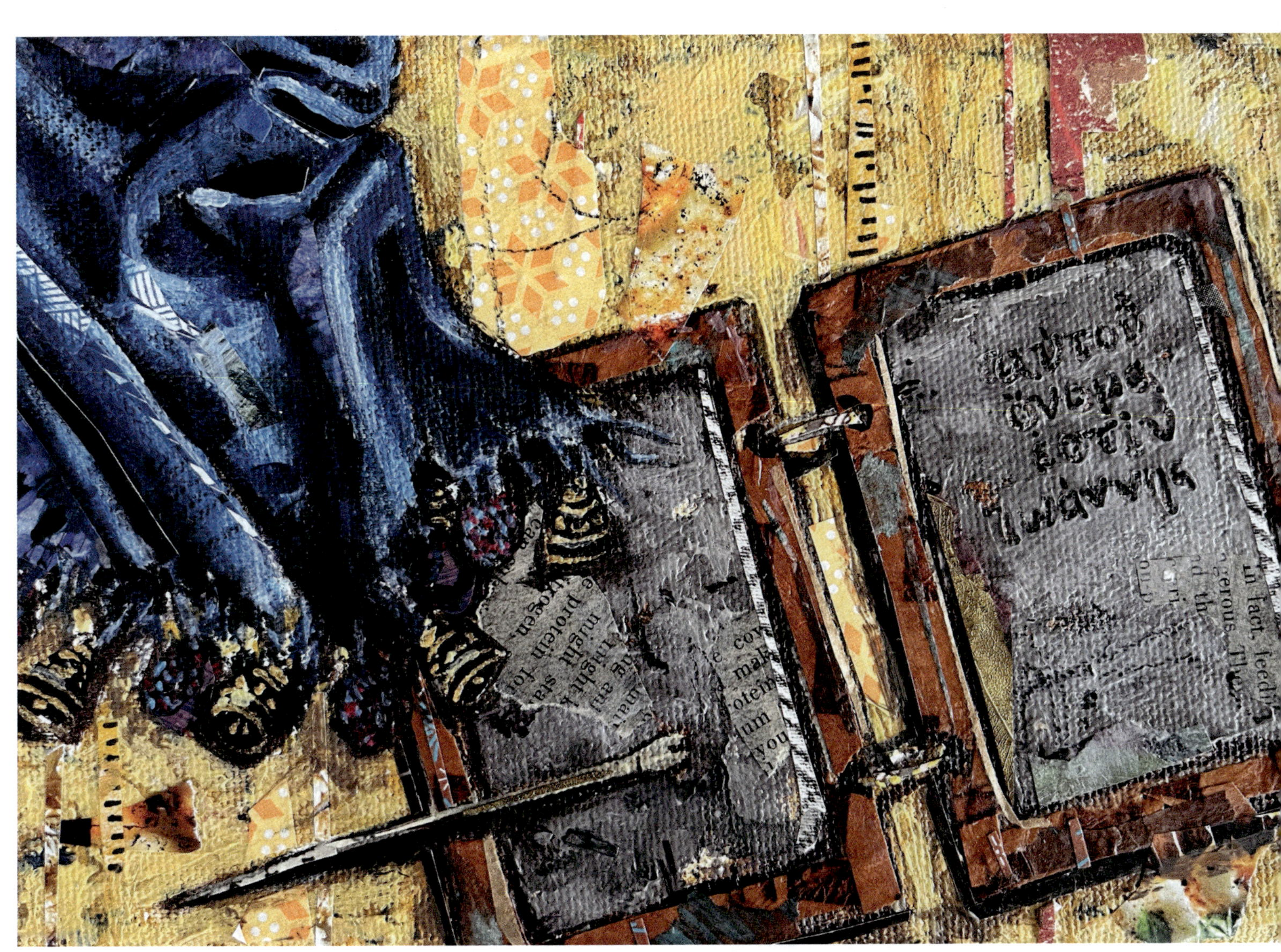
αὐτοῦ
ὄνομα
ἐστίν
Ἰωάννης

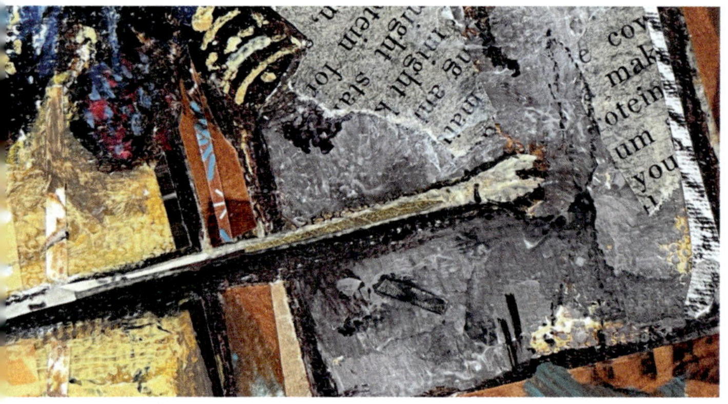

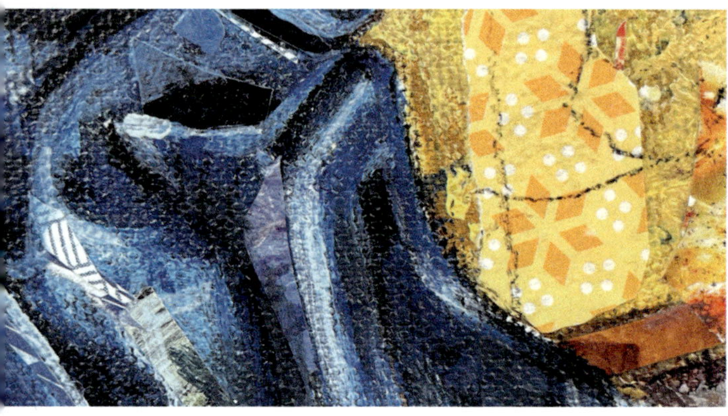

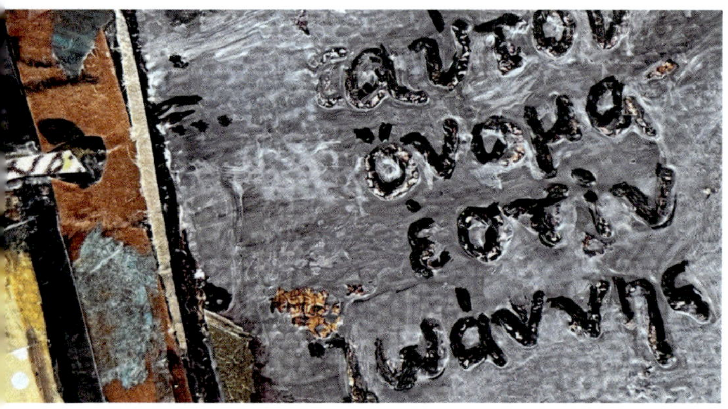

Empires rose and fell,
and still no messiah had come.
But Rome,
it claimed the savior of the world
was on their throne.
Israel, still resisting the iron fist.
Caesar insisting they comply.
Even the temple bore the stamp
of whose hand was divine.
Zechariah, a priest of old age
who walked in the way of Aaron
(the first high priest),
his wife Elizabeth was barren,
so they would parent the flock instead.
By lot he was chosen
to travel to Jerusalem
and enter the holy place.
On the altar he'd lay the incense
and offer the prayers of the people there.
The sweet fragrance would fill the temple,
as he'd ask the Father
to cover the stench of their sins.
But when he went in, an angel stood near.
Zechariah trembled in fear.
"Do not be afraid.
Elizabeth will have a son.
You'll call him John.
He'll make ready the way for the Lord."

Dumb-founded Zechariah dared to ask,
"How can I know that this is true?"
And the angel made him mute,
unable to speak
because he did not believe
the miracle God would do.
The altered priest would use his hands to sign,
until the time
his wife gave birth to their son.
The family insisted on the father's name,
but Zechariah wouldn't have it.
He took the writing tablet and wrote out,
"His name is John!"
Gabriel's words he would keep,
and in belief he was made to speak again,
holding in his hands
the one who'd cry in the desert.
Zechariah would wipe away the tears,
whisper into John's ear,
"You, my son,
prophet of the Highest One.
You will prepare the way
for the Messiah
who comes to save."

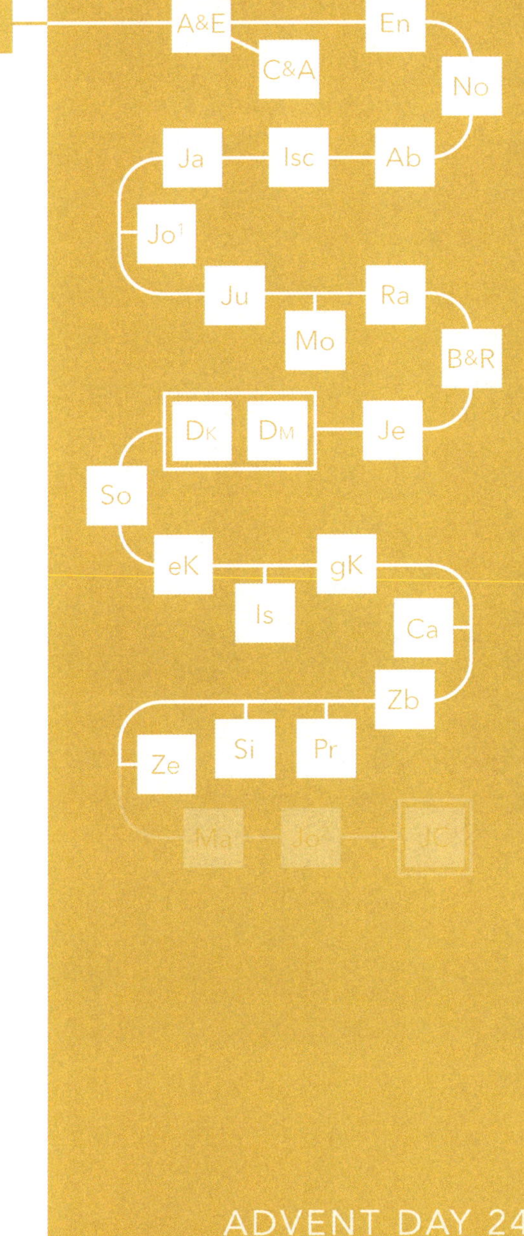

ADVENT DAY 24
ZECHARIAH

25

MARY

She treasured up all these things, pondering them in her heart.

FROM THE SCRIPTURE, GOD TELLS HIS STORY...

LUKE 1:26-38, 46-55

The angel Gabriel was sent from God to a city of Galilee named Nazareth, to a virgin betrothed to a man whose name was Joseph, of the house of David. And the virgin's name was Mary. And he came to her and said, "Greetings, O favored one, the Lord is with you!" But she was greatly troubled at the saying, and tried to discern what sort of greeting this might be. And the angel said to her, "Do not be afraid, Mary, for you have found favor with God. And behold, you will conceive in your womb and bear a son, and you shall call his name Jesus. He will be great and will be called the Son of the Most High. And the Lord God will give to him the throne of his father David, and he will reign over the house of Jacob forever, and of his kingdom there will be no end."

And Mary said to the angel, "How will this be, since I am a virgin?" And the angel answered her, "The Holy Spirit will come upon you, and the power of the Most High will overshadow you; therefore the child to be born will be called holy — the Son of God. And behold, your relative Elizabeth in her old age has also conceived a son, and this is the sixth month with her who was called barren. For nothing will be impossible with God."

And Mary said, "Behold, I am the servant of the Lord; let it be to me according to your word." And the angel departed from her.

... And Mary said,

"My soul magnifies the Lord, and my spirit rejoices in God my Savior,
for he has looked on the humble estate of his servant.
For behold, from now on all generations will call me blessed;
for he who is mighty has done great things for me, and holy is his name.
And his mercy is for those who fear him from generation to generation.
He has shown strength with his arm;
he has scattered the proud in the thoughts of their hearts;
he has brought down the mighty from their thrones
and exalted those of humble estate;
he has filled the hungry with good things,
and the rich he has sent away empty.
He has helped his servant Israel, in remembrance of his mercy,
as he spoke to our fathers, to Abraham and to his offspring forever."

Mary visits Elizabeth (Luke 1:39-45, 56)

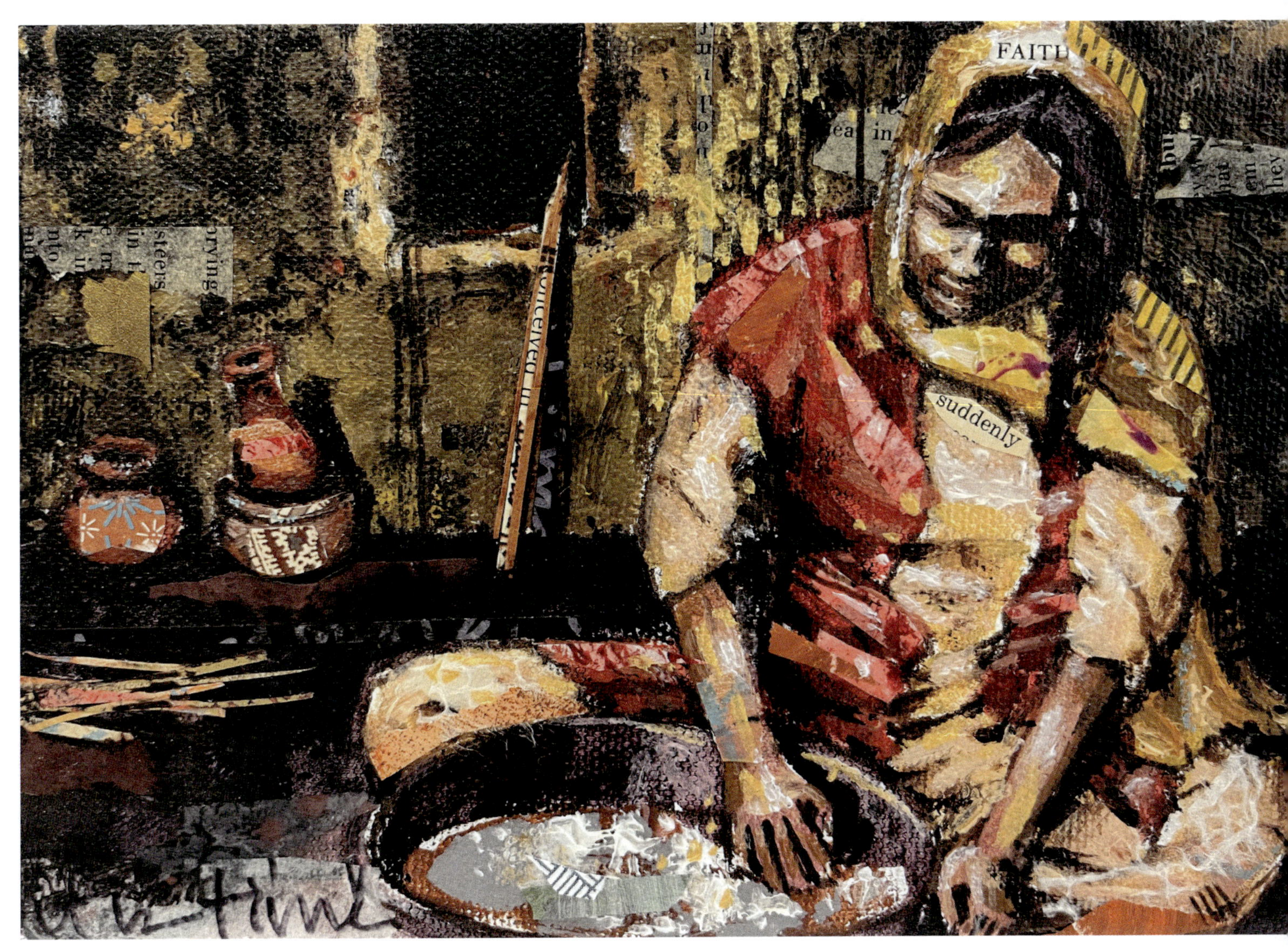
FAITH
suddenly

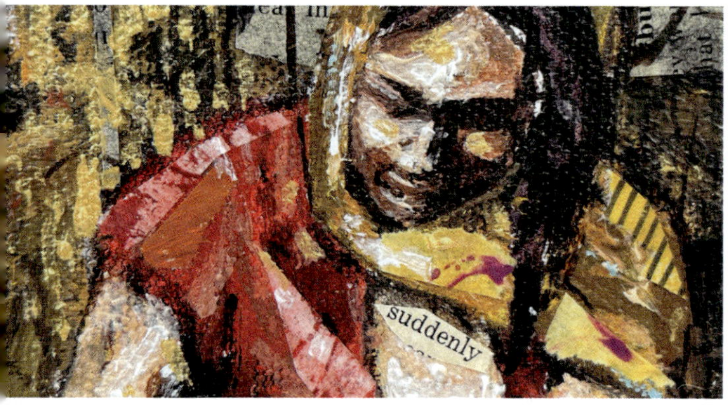

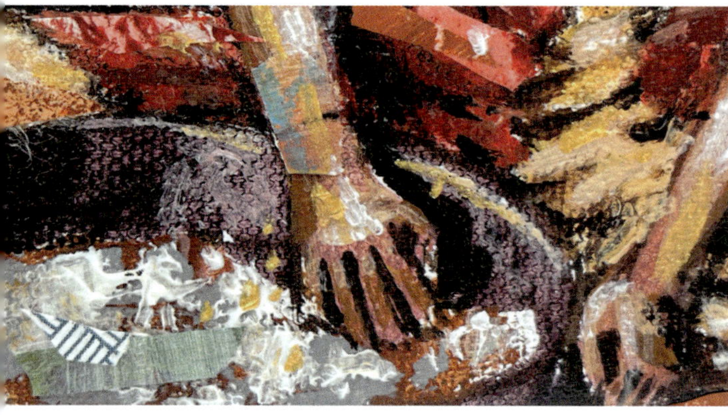

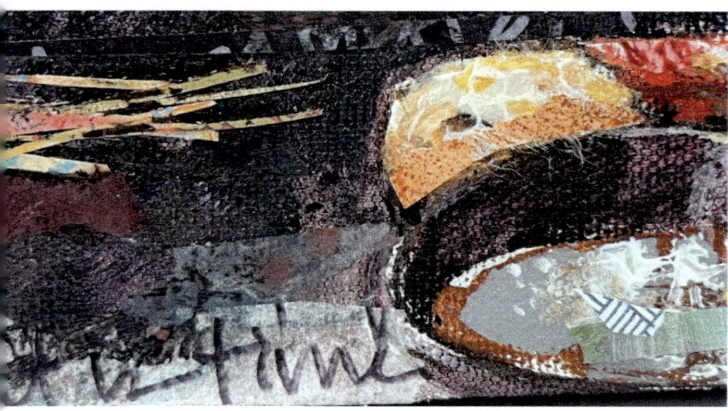

A poor young girl engaged,
waiting for the day
when a covenant would be made
with a righteous man
who would keep her and bless.
What happened next would cause certain unrest
to all those she knew.
Joseph too.
Gabriel was sent to address
a girl no one guessed would be chosen.
"Greetings favored one!
The Lord has come near."
Fear.
Unprepared and surprised,
her humble eyes would turn away
to see clearly what had been said.
"Do not be afraid, Mary,
for you carry a son,
the only begotten One
of the Most High.
He will be great and will take David's throne
and reign a kingdom with no end."
Mary picking up the pieces of her plan
asked how it could be
if she'd not known a man in this way.

Gabriel would say,
“God’s Spirit will overshadow
what can-not-be
and place the seed
(the one foretold from the garden of old)
into your womb to grow.”

Soon she’d show
and they would know
and she’d confess this encounter.
Among all women, God had found her
to carry His Son.

Mary would sing,
“My soul magnifies my God,
my King.
He has done great things for me
and for those of every generation,
of every nation, who fear Him.
He scatters the proud and brings them down
but lifts up the servant
and crowns her with mercy.”
And Mary, fulfilling her part,
would ponder these things in her heart
all her son’s days.

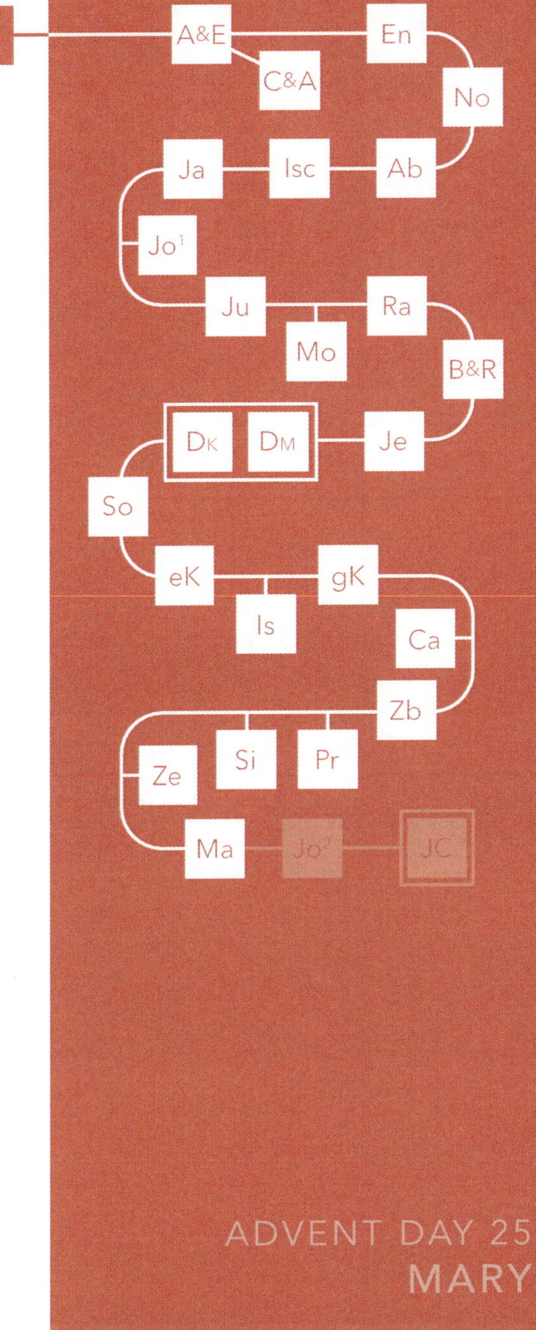

26

JOSEPH, HUSBAND OF MARY

Joseph, son of David, do not fear to take Mary as your wife.

FROM SCRIPTURE, GOD TELLS HIS STORY...

MATTHEW 1:18-25

Now the birth of Jesus Christ took place in this way. When his mother Mary had been betrothed to Joseph, before they came together she was found to be with child from the Holy Spirit. And her husband Joseph, being a just man and unwilling to put her to shame, resolved to divorce her quietly. But as he considered these things, behold, an angel of the Lord appeared to him in a dream, saying, "Joseph, son of David, do not fear to take Mary as your wife, for that which is conceived in her is from the Holy Spirit. She will bear a son, and you shall call his name Jesus, for he will save his people from their sins." All this took place to fulfill what the Lord had spoken by the prophet:

"Behold, the virgin shall conceive and bear a son, and they shall call his name Immanuel" (which means, God with us). When Joseph woke from sleep, he did as the angel of the Lord commanded him: he took his wife, but knew her not until she had given birth to a son.

LUKE 2:1-4

In those days a decree went out from Caesar Augustus that all the world should be registered. This was the first registration when Quirinius was governor of Syria. And all went to be registered, each to his own town. And Joseph also went up from Galilee, from the town of Nazareth, to Judea, to the city of David, which is called Bethlehem, because he was of the house and lineage of David.

MATTHEW 13:55

"Is not this the carpenter's son? Is not his mother called Mary?"

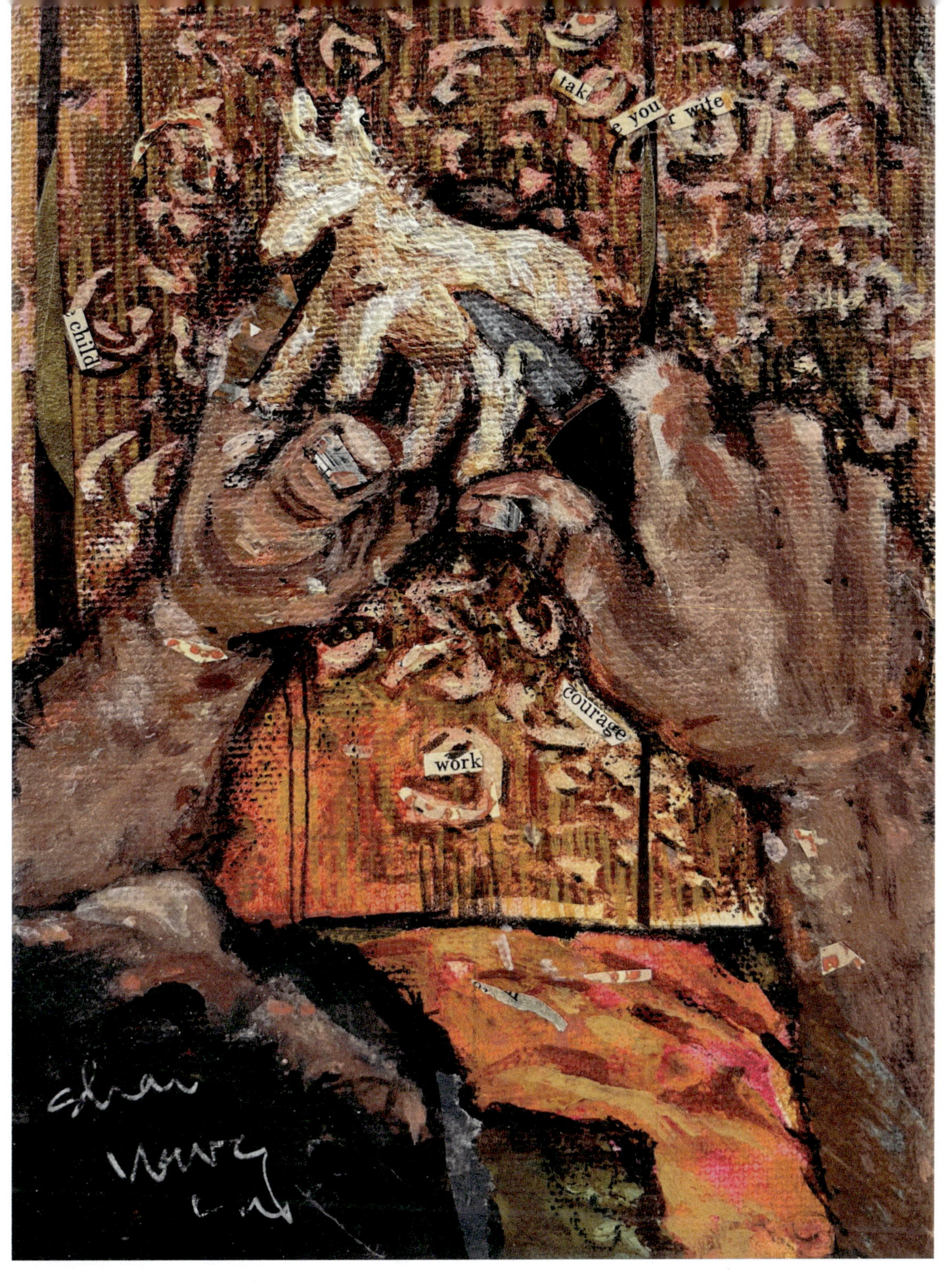
child
courage
work

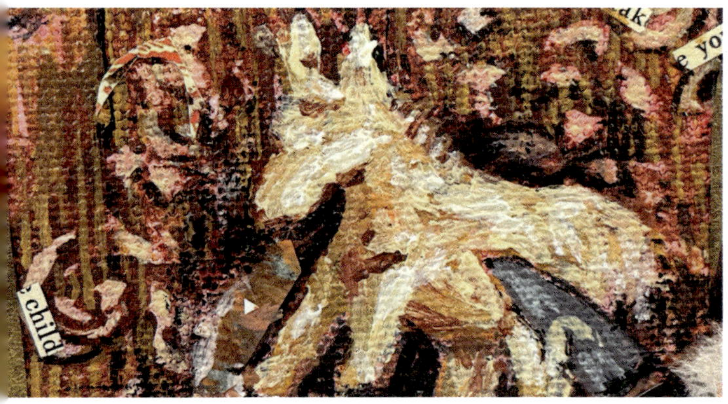

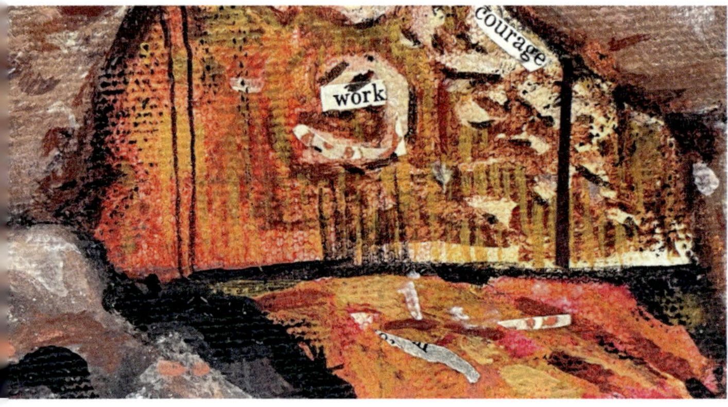

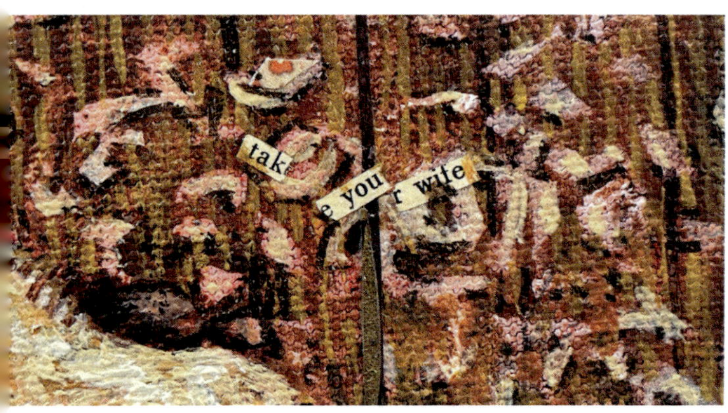

Joseph,
a carpenter by trade.
He made things
by his own two hands,
and those things had *plans.*
His fiancé was expecting.
It's the last thing Joseph expected.
He inspected Mary's face for reason.
Tension danced between them.
Wrestling with what she explained.
Turning it over and over in his head.
Who would believe they had not sinned
or that Mary had not been with another
and was trying to cover her misstep?
Joseph had promised forever,
but never imagined
they'd weather this storm.
Torn.
It seemed best to send her away
and preserve any honor left to their name.

Night came.
God would orient his spinning heart.
An angel called out his name.
"Joseph,
of David's line,
You will find
what Mary said is right.

Take her as your wife
without fear or shame.
You will name him Jesus.
Her son has come to save."

The Light would wake him
to marry Mary
and bury the doubt.
He found his compass not spinning about,
but pointing one way.
Didn't have to know how,
just needed to obey.
And piece by piece,
God would whittle away
at a *plan*
that would bring them peace.

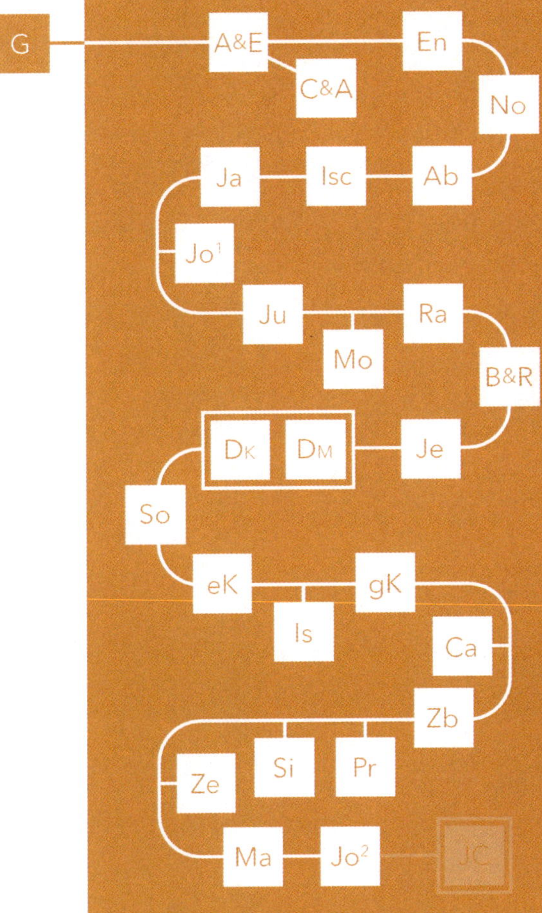

ADVENT DAY 26

JOSEPH, HUSBAND OF MARY

27

JESUS

When the fullness of time had come, God sent forth his Son.

FROM SCRIPTURE, GOD TELLS HIS STORY...

Kiss the Son (Psalm 2)

LUKE 2:3-20

And all went to be registered, each to his own town. And Joseph also went up from Galilee, from the town of Nazareth, to Judea, to the city of David, which is called Bethlehem, because he was of the house and lineage of David, to be registered with Mary, his betrothed, who was with child. And while they were there, the time came for her to give birth. And she gave birth to her firstborn son and wrapped him in swaddling cloths and laid him in a manger, because there was no place for them in the inn.

And in the same region there were shepherds out in the field, keeping watch over their flock by night. And an angel of the Lord appeared to them, and the glory of the Lord shone around them, and they were filled with great fear. And the angel said to them, "Fear not, for behold, I bring you good news of great joy that will be for all the people. For unto you is born this day in the city of David a Savior, who is Christ the Lord. And this will be a sign for you: you will find a baby wrapped in swaddling cloths and lying in a manger." And suddenly there was with the angel a multitude of the heavenly host praising God and saying,

"Glory to God in the highest, and on earth peace among those with whom he is pleased!"

When the angels went away from them into heaven, the shepherds said to one another, "Let us go over to Bethlehem and see this thing that has happened, which the Lord has made known to us." And they went with haste and found Mary and Joseph, and the baby lying in a manger. And when they saw it, they made known the saying that had been told them concerning this child. And all who heard it wondered at what the shepherds told them. But Mary treasured up all these things, pondering them in her heart. And the shepherds returned, glorifying and praising God for all they had heard and seen, as it had been told them.

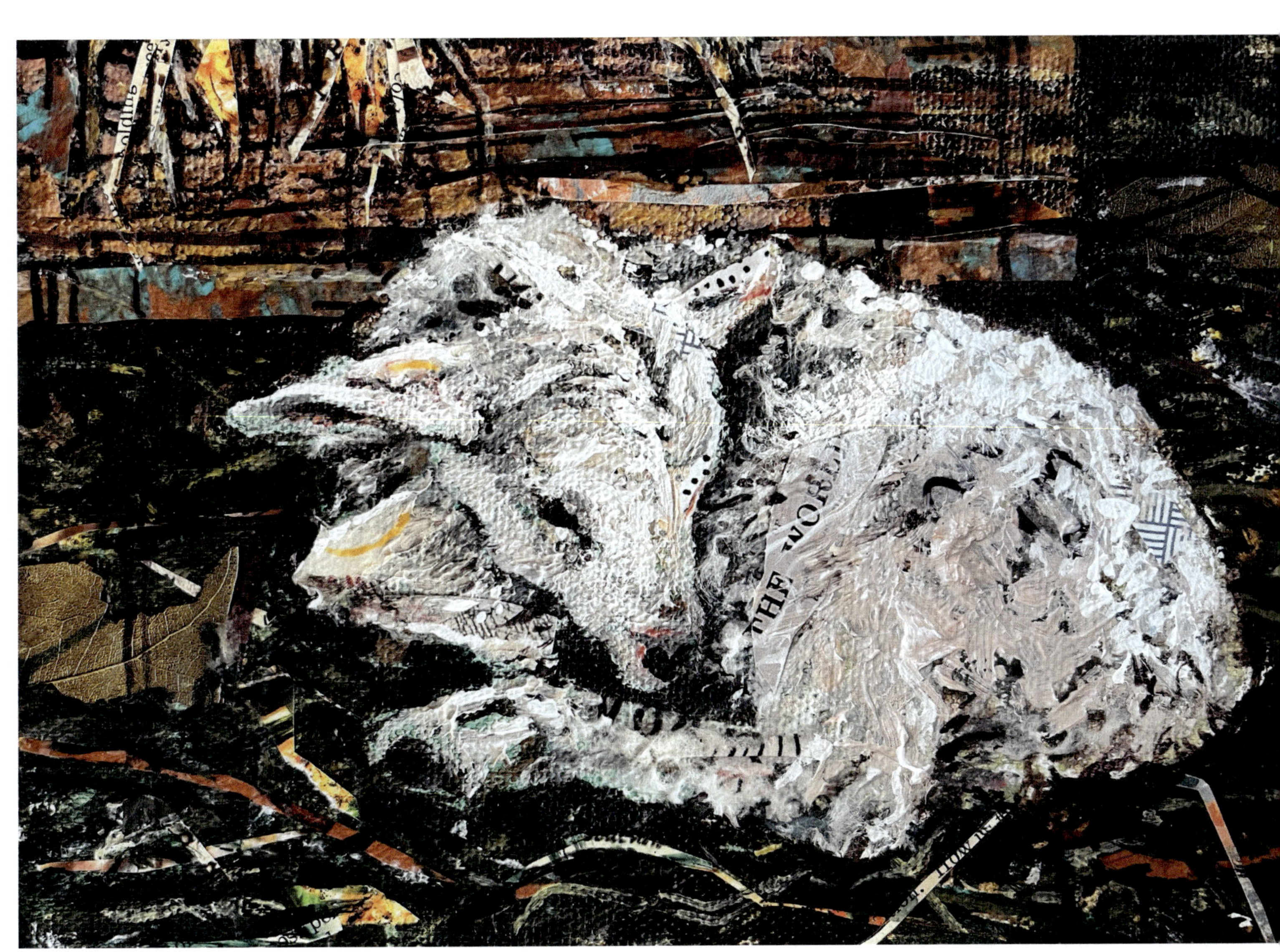

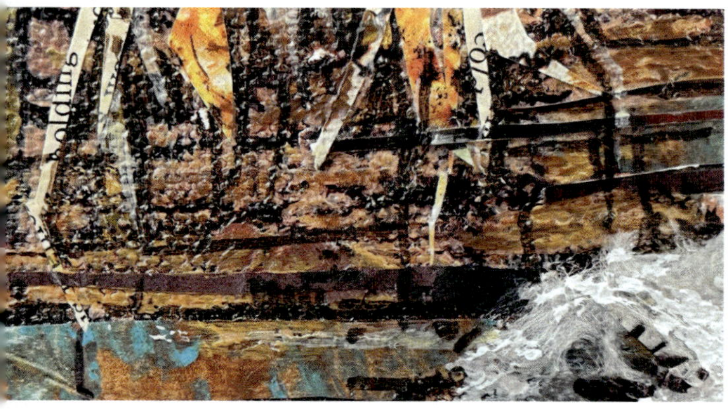

Behold, Caesar Augustus,
son of Julius,
"Son of the god."
Rome would worship and claim
he was *the beginning of good tidings*
for the world.
"A savior," they said in vain.
But God would laugh —
"I have installed My king."

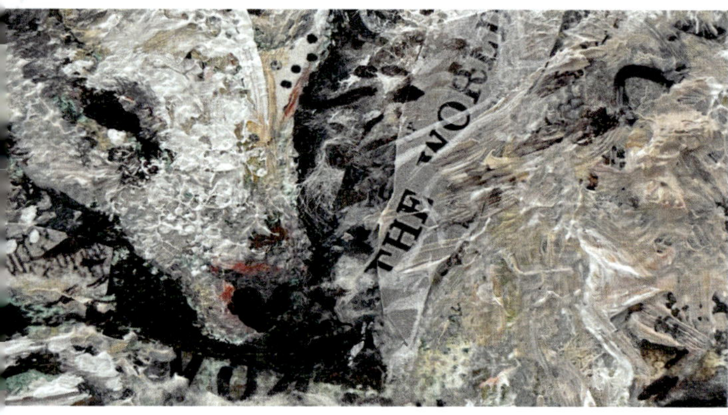

Behold, Joseph and Mary
traveling on foot.
Her days to carry her son
were about to end,
but Caesar would send them
to David's town.
No room was found for them.
But God had not forgotten —
"You are My Son;
today I have begotten you."

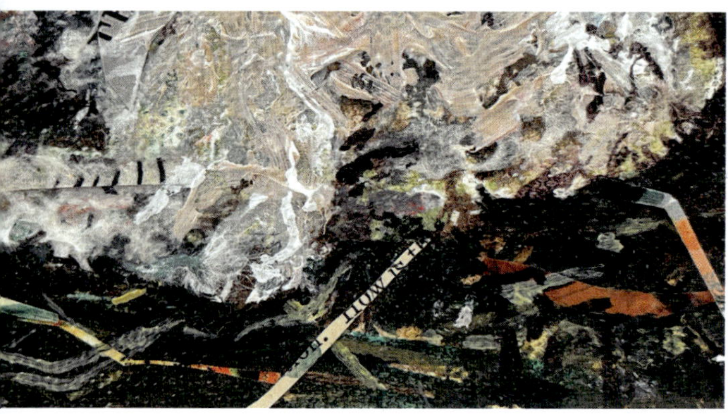

Behold, shepherds nearby
keeping watch over sheep.
An angel would speak,
"Fear not!
Tidings of great joy for all mankind!"
He gave a sign to where they would find
this one like *them.*

Shepherd to shepherd.
Unclean to unseen.
But God knew who he was sending —
"Serve your Lord with fear and trembling."

Behold, a host of angels
filling the sky.
Oh, what a sight that night!
Mary, Joseph, and the newborn son
hidden in the town,
found by shepherds flocking in,
gathering 'round.
Oh, what a humble thing
to be at the foot of the King.

Behold, the Lamb of God
who takes away our sin.
Son of God.
Son of Man.
"Kiss the Son.
Blessed are all
who take refuge in Him."

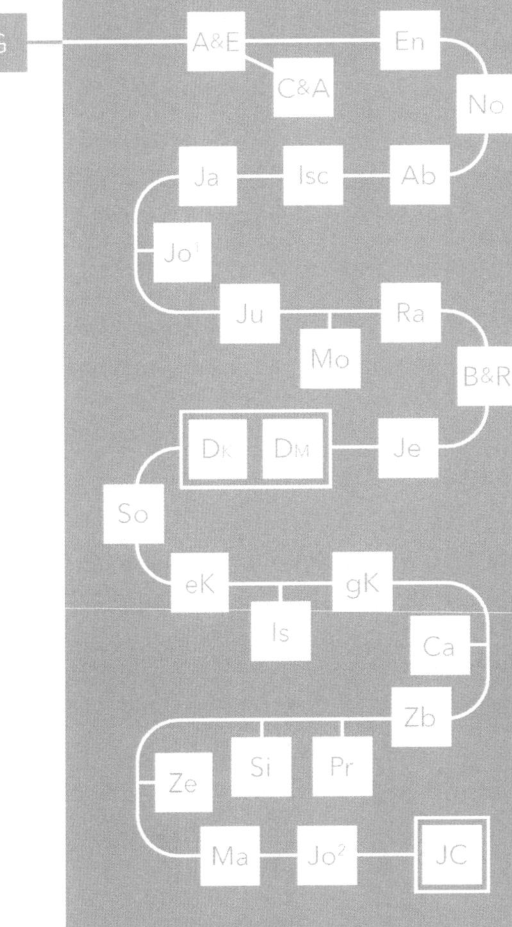

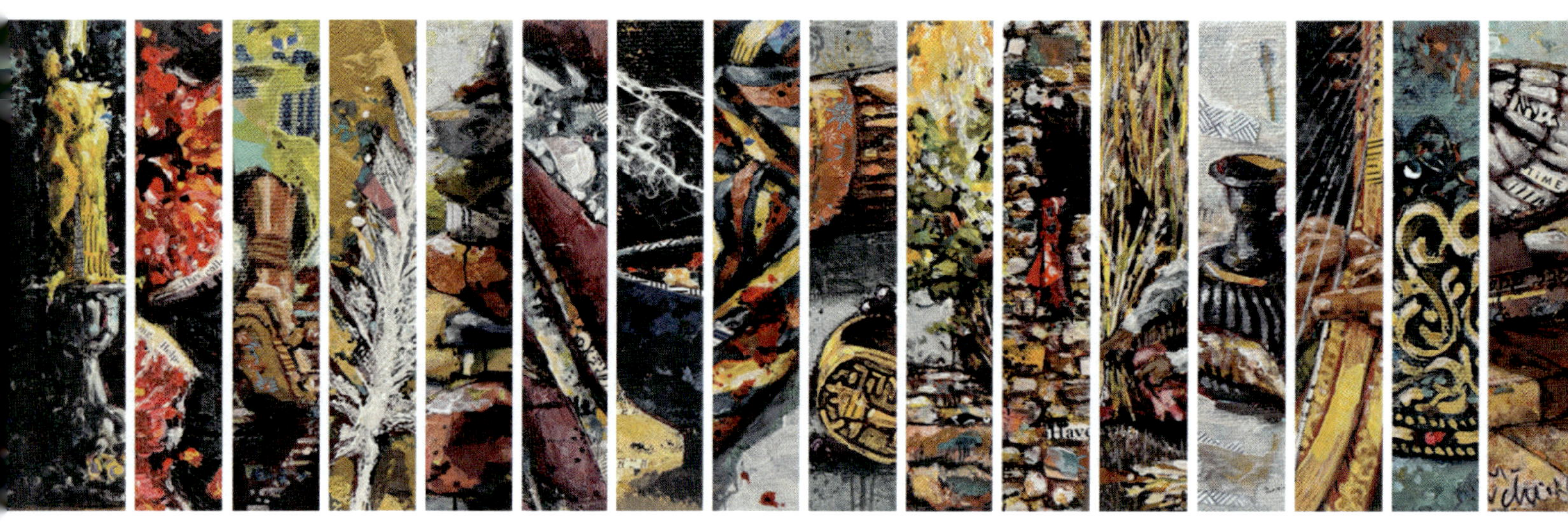

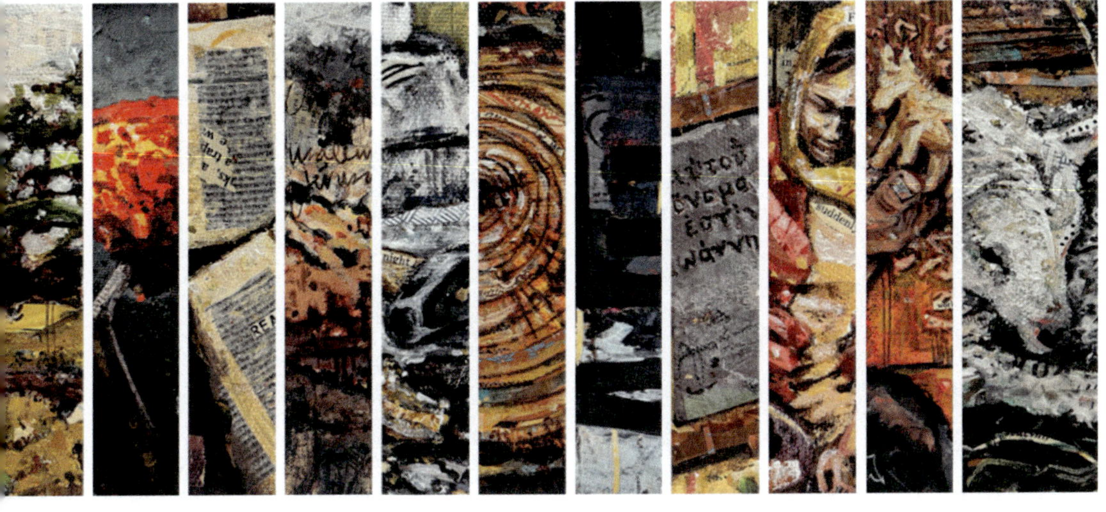

The people
who walked in darkness
have seen a great light;
those who dwelt in a land
of deep darkness,
on them has light shone.
ISAIAH 9:2

ACKNOWLEDGMENTS

This book is dedicated to the Messiah, the Beginning and End of the full story, whose beauty is more than I could ever paint or write. To orient these gifts to your glory is both my delight and freedom. Your story and creation provide endless inspiration.

I'm grateful for my husband and kids who brought me cups and cups of coffee, looked over my shoulder, and graciously honored the time required for me to work every day through the Advent season. Their support and love is integrated into every day's endeavor.

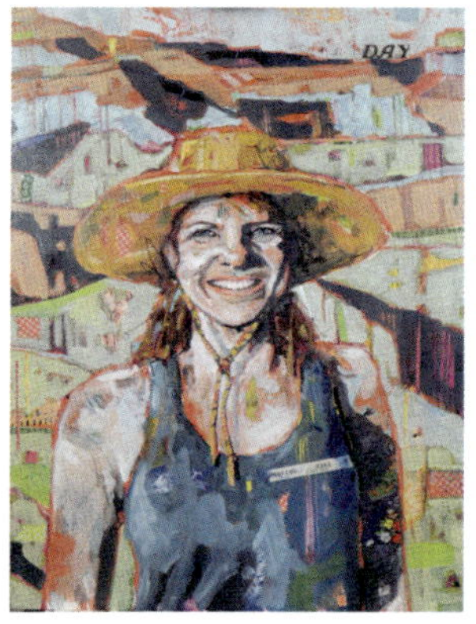

ABOUT THE ARTIST & AUTHOR

Riki Yarbrough is an artist, graphic designer, writer, and lover of the outdoors. Because her creative process is centered on her own sojourn, her mixed media work is content-rich, personal, and seeps themes of faith, Scripture, struggle, womanhood, motherhood, and the beautiful landscapes she's hiked. At home she is a wife to Jeremy and mom to Micah, Payton, and Grayson.

Made in the USA
Las Vegas, NV
09 November 2024